80 HANDMADE GIFTS:
Year-Round Projects to Cook, Crochet, Knit, Sew & More!

by Kristin Omdahl

EDITORS: Karen Blumberg, Grace Cieply, and Judi Weingarden

COVER AND INTERIOR DESIGN: Kristin Omdahl

PHOTOGRAPHERS: Marlon Omdahl and Kristin Omdahl

ILLUSTRATION: Kristin Omdahl

@ 2018 Kristin Omdahl
All rights reserved

Kristin Omdahl
18780 Trade Way Four
Ste 107-301
Bonita Springs, FL 34135
KristinOmdahl.com

Manufactured in USA

Library of Congress Cataloging-in-Publication Data
Omdahl, Kristin.
80 Handmade Gifts: Year-Round Projects to Cook, Crochet, Knit, Sew & More!

Includes index
ISBN-13: 9781728620183

1. Crocheting -- Patterns. 2. Knitting -- Patterns. 3. Sewing -- Patterns. 4. Cooking -- Recipes.

TABLE OF CONTENTS

Acknowledgements 3
Dedication 3
Introduction 3
Recipes
   Granola 4
   Chai Spice 5
   Spiced Nuts 6
   Baklava Balls 7
   Toffee 8
   Simple Syrups 9
   Garlic Infused Oil 10
   Fruit Vinegar 11
   Lemon Blueberry Mini Loaf Cakes 12
   Lime Raspberry Loaf Cake 12
   Orange Cardamom Mini Muffins 12
   Sweet Pickled Relish 14
   Moroccan Pickled Carrots. 14
   Asian Pickled Green Beans 14
   Truffles 16
   Cheese Log 17
   Cheese Crackers 18
   Quinoa Crackers 19
   Cashew Cream 20
   Cocoa Mixes 21
   Flavored Sugars 22
   Peach Chutney 23
Crochet
   Marlene Bag 24
   Hope Case 27
   Abigail Bag 29
   Jennifer Bowl 31
   Belle Napkin 33
   Cami Scarf 34
   Celeste Earrings 35
   Olivia Shawl 36
   Felicia Mobius Cowl 38
   Lexi Washcloth 39
   Kate Trivet 41
   Sami Trivet 43
   Nicole Washcloth 45
   Mimi Candle Holder 47
   Melanie Candle Holder ... 49
   Caroline Candle Holder .. 51
   Gabi Candle Holder 53
   Grace Bracelet 55
   Rachel Necklace 56
   Amanda Necklace 57
   Liz Necklace 58
   Kelly Earrings 59
   Tanya Jar Topper 60
   Dana Earrings 62
Knitting
   Maggie Bag 63
   Caliope Bag 65
   Carrie Bag 66
   Courtney Bowl 67
   Carly Napkin 68
   Ciara Scarf 69
   Arianna Earrings 70
   Kimberly Necklace Cowl 71
   Nina Shawl 72
   Iris Mobius Cowl 73
   Chelsea Washcloth 74
   Khloe Bowl 75
   Vivian Small Basket 76
   Cassie Medium Basket .. 77
   Eve Large Basket 78
   Lani Jar Topper 79
   Mia Bracelet 80
   Donna Necklace 81
   Paulina Necklace 82
   Bridget Bracelet 83
Sewing, Paper Crafts & More
   Eden Card 84
   Julia Card 85
   Lenora Card 86
   Gina Card 87
   Sophia Box 88
   Augusta Basket 90
   Henrietta Box 91
   Victoria Box 93
   Cassandra Box 95
   Pearl Apron 96
   Heather Roll 98
   Reese Bag 99
   Sasha Stitch Markers .. 101
   Emily Eye Pillow 102
   Alice Bag 103
   Annie Pouch 104
   Ada Roll 105
   Margot Pouch 106
   Greta Bath Bombs 107
Symbol Library 108
Glossaries 108, 109
Project Kristin Cares 110
Resources 110
Index 111

Dedication

This book is dedicated to Marlon. No matter what life has in store for us, we will always have each other. We share a dedication to hard work and staying focused on our goals. You inspire me every day to laugh and have more fun along the way. I am so proud of you. I love you with all my heart and soul.

Acknowledgements

Thank you to Karen Blumberg, Grace Cieply, and Judi Weingarden for your impeccable attention to details. Thank you to my podcast audience for sharing your enthusiasm and feedback with me every day.

Introduction

As far back as I can remember, long before I was even a crafting professional, I have been creating one-of-a-kind gifts by hand. In addition to making sure that the gift would be useful, I was customizing ideas for a particular person to make sure that the gift had special or hidden meanings in the type of craft, color or content of materials. Creating a gift by hand displays your most heartfelt feelings and is almost magical. I have had a lifetime of opportunities to share my enthusiasm for creating through gifting, teaching, and empowering others to create, teach, gift and sell their own handmade creations.

The focus of this collection is simple and quick handmade crafts. Many of the projects are kid-friendly for teaching our love of creating to family and empowering the next generation of crafters. There is a focus on quick gifts in relation to labor cost for those interested in selling their handmade items. This collection of projects was curated with usefulness in mind: a gift that can be used regularly is a gift that keeps on giving.

While the most common purpose of handmade gifts is holidays, I think having a go-to reference of quick and easy crafts makes handmade gifting possible for so many other opportunities: appreciation of an act of kindness; pick-me-up for a friend; last minute invite to a party; or no reason at all.

Learning is such a personal experience and each of us learns in a unique way. Please enjoy the written instructions, charts, schematics and the supplemental video tutorials on my website to enhance your experience. This entire book is printed in larger font to make reading it as simple and easy as possible.

I am so excited to share **80 Handmade Gifts** with you. I hope you enjoy creating and sharing this collection as much as I do!

CHAI SPICED GRANOLA

Homemade granola is rich and nutrient dense. This recipe can easily be made in large batches, allowing you to prepare many gifts at one time.

What you will need:

Simple Syrup:
- 2 cups light brown sugar
- 2 cups water

Granola:
- 3 TBSP chai spice (see recipe page 5)
- 1 tsp freshly grated ginger
- 8 cups rolled oats
- 4 cups chopped pecans
- 4 cups slivered almonds
- 2 cups sweetened shredded coconut
- 2 cups dried fruits (I used cranberries and pineapple)

Yield: This recipes makes 12 cups of granola.

Instructions:
Granola:

1. Preheat oven to 350 F degrees.

2. Make chai spice (see page 5).

3. Make simple syrup: mix the sugar and water together over medium heat. Stir until sugar is dissolved. Stir in the chai spice mix and freshly grated ginger. Simmer for 2 more minutes.

4. Strain sugar syrup through strainer and set aside.

5. In a large mixing bowl, combine oatmeal, nuts and coconut. Drizzle with spiced sugar syrup and mix everything together.

6. Spread granola on a 13 in (33cm) x 18 in (45cm) baking sheet. Bake in oven for 60 minutes, stirring every 20 minutes.

7. Allow to cool completely before mixing in the dried fruit. Break up any large clumps.

8. Transfer to gift bags, boxes or jars.

Will keep in airtight container for up to one month.

Note: Omit the chai spice for a simpler flavor.

CHAI SPICE MIX

Chai spice is a heady, exotic blend of warm spices that are so comforting in a tea latte. But don't stop there! This mix is amazing in baked goods and all sorts of sweet and savory foods, too. Gift a spice jar filled with this exotic blend, a pretty mug and a tea diffuser.

What you will need:

- 1 TBSP black pepper, ground
- 6 TBSPS dried cinnamon, ground
- 6 TBSPS dried ginger, ground
- 4 star anise pods
- 6 whole cloves
- 10 green cardamom pods

Yield: three 2oz (56g) spice jars

Instructions:

1. Pulse star anise, cloves and cardamom pods in blender or food processor until finely ground. If you prefer, grind by hand using a mortar and pestle.

2. Add remaining ingredients and pulse until combined.

Store in an air tight container for six months.

Note: Steep in black tea for chai spiced tea or steep in any liquid to add chai seasoning to baked goods.

Be sure to strain after steeping; the spices will scent the liquid and the bits should be discarded. This is very strong and spicy. Start with 1/2 tsp for making tea and increase as desired.

Use it to spice pudding, custard, cakes, muffins, granola, lattes, teas or candied nuts. It is a potent spice blend: a little goes a long way!

SPICED NUTS

Sweet & salty, spiced nuts with an egg white coating contain only a minimal amount of sugar, and no oil or butter. These wonderfully spiced, crunchy nuts are easy to make. Who wouldn't appreciate such a healthy and delicious gift?

What you will need:

- 1 cup cashews
- 1 cup almonds
- 1 cup macadamias
- 1 cup pistachios
- 2 egg whites
- 1/2 cup light brown sugar
- 1-1/2 tsp Himalayan pink salt, fine grind
- 1 tsp cinnamon, ground
- 1 tsp cumin, ground
- 1 tsp chili powder
- 1 tsp smoked paprika
- 1/2 tsp ginger, ground
- 1/4 tsp cloves, ground
- 1/4 tsp cayenne pepper

Yield: This recipe makes 4 cups of spiced nuts.

Instructions:

1. Preheat oven to 250 F degrees.

2. Mix all spices together. Add sugar and egg whites. Whisk together for 2 minutes until sugar dissolves.

3. Add nuts and coat evenly.

4. Pour nuts onto parchment paper lined, rimmed cookie sheet.

5. Bake in oven for 60 minutes, stirring every 20 minutes.

6. Allow to cool completely.

For gifts, use jars, tins, pastry boxes or other creative containers and decorate with a bow. Otherwise store in an airtight container for up to one month.

BAKLAVA

No Bake Energy Balls

Only 5 ingredients, no baking, and it takes less than 10 minutes to make a whole batch. These energy balls include the flavors of baklava, my all time favorite dessert. At about 150 calories per ball, these are a healthier indulgence than traditional baklava.

What you will need:

- 2 cups chopped, toasted walnuts
- 2 cups pitted dates
- 1 cup shredded coconut, unsweetened
- 1 TBSP cinnamon, ground
- 1 TBSP rose water

Yield: This recipe makes twenty 1 inch (25cm) balls.

Instructions:

Note: Walnuts should be toasted in a 300 F oven for about 10 - 15 minutes (or until fragrant), and then allowed to cool completely before being used.

1. Combine all ingredients in food processor.

2. Pulse until ingredients combine and pull away from the sides.

3. Wet hands so the mixture doesn't stick. Roll it into 1 inch (25cm) balls.

4. Refrigerate for at least an hour.

5. Store in an airtight container for up to one week.

TOFFEE

This is outrageously delicious and easier to make than you might think. Buy your nuts at a bulk store to keep the cost down.

What you will need:

- 2 cups salted or unsalted mixed nuts or any nuts that you prefer
- 1 cup chopped pecans
- 2 cups semi-sweet chocolate chips
- 1 cup butter, salted
- 1 cup organic cane sugar (regular sugar can be substituted)
- Candy thermometer

Yield: This recipe makes approximately four cups, more or less, depending on size of shards.

Instructions:

1. Spread mixed nuts evenly across an ungreased cookie sheet. Do not add pecans at this stage.

2. Melt butter in a medium saucepan on high heat. Add sugar and stir constantly with a wooden spoon.

3. When the mixture starts bubbling, turn heat to medium and continue to stir constantly for 10 - 13 minutes, or until mixture turns light golden brown. (Must read 300 F on candy thermometer).

4. Quickly pour toffee mixture over the nuts on the cookie sheet. Move quickly as it begins to harden faster than you might think.

5. Sprinkle chocolate chips over the top. Allow to sit for 3 - 5 minutes, then smooth the melted chocolate over the entire tray of toffee.

6. Sprinkle chopped pecans over the top.

7. Cool in refrigerator until completely hardened and set.

8. Break into shard-like pieces; smaller for a serving platter or larger for a gift box.

SIMPLE SYRUPS

Flavored simple syrups are an incredibly easy way to add depth and surprising flavor to lemonades, baked goods, coffee drinks, and so much more.

From left to right: banana, lavender, blueberry, rose, lemon, orange

Note: The basic ratio for simple syrup is 1 part sugar to 1 part water, but when adding flavors, the ratio can change depending on the moisture content of the flavoring ingredients.

What you will need:

Banana Simple Syrup:
- 3 ripe bananas
- 1 cup sugar
- 1/2 cup water

Lavender Simple Syrup:
- 1 cup sugar
- 1 cup water
- 2 TBSP dried lavender buds
- 1 drop purple food coloring (optional)

Blueberry Simple Syrup:
- 1 cup sugar
- 1/2 cup water
- 1 cup fresh blueberries

Rose Simple Syrup:
- 1 cup sugar
- 1 cup water
- 1 cup dried organic rose petals

Lemon Simple Syrup:
- 1 cup sugar
- 1 cup water
- zest and juice of 2 lemons

Orange Simple Syrup:
- 1 cup sugar
- 1 cup water
- zest and juice of 2 oranges

Instructions:

1. Pour sugar and water into a pot on the stove, bring to a simmer and stir until dissolved.

2. Remove from heat and add flavorings to your syrup. Allow to steep as the liquid cools.

3. Strain flavors out of the syrup.

4. Pour cooled, flavored syrup into a sealable bottle or jar.

Flavored simple syrup will last up to one month in the refrigerator.

GARLIC INFUSED OIL

Flavor infused oils are fantastic to keep on hand for adding depth of flavor to vinaigrettes, marinades, breads, sauces and more. They also make a great last minute gift that can be whipped up in just a few minutes. Present with a fresh loaf of bread for a gift that can be added right to the dinner table!

What you will need:

- 3 cups extra virgin olive oil
- 4 cloves garlic, crushed

Option 1:
add 1 sprig fresh rosemary

Option 2:
add 2 - 3 sprigs fresh oregano

Option 3:
add 2 - 3 sprigs fresh thyme

Option 3:
add 1/2 tsp red chili flakes

Yield: This recipe makes 3 cups of oil.

Instructions:

1. Add oil and garlic to pot on stove.

2. Heat to a simmer. Allow to cool.

Note: if adding herbs, add them to the oil while it is still hot. Steeping brings out the flavors.

3. Strain garlic (and any herbs) from oil.

4. Pour into sealable bottles. Add a clove of garlic to the bottle. If you added herbs to the oil, add a fresh sprig of that herb to the bottles for decoration.

Will last in a cool, dark location for one month.

VINEGARS
Fruit Flavored

Fruit flavored vinegars add so much depth and variety to your recipes. Easily swap out vinegar for any vinaigrette, marinade or recipe with a fruit flavored vinegar.

What you will need:

- 3 cups white wine vinegar
- 1 cup fresh raspberries

Option 2:
- 3 cups white wine vinegar
- 2 cups fresh peaches, diced

Option 3:
- 3 cups white wine vinegar
- 1 cup fresh strawberries

Option 4:
- 3 cups white vinegar
- zest of 3 lemons
- 1 bunch of fresh thyme

Option 4:
- 3 cups white vinegar
- zest of 3 oranges
- 1 clove garlic, thinly sliced

Instructions:

1. Add vinegar and raspberries to pot on stove.

2. Heat to a simmer. Allow to cool.

3. Strain seeds from liquid.

4. Pour into sealable bottles.

Will last in a cool, dark place for up to one month or two to three months in the refrigerator.

Lemon Blueberry Mini Loaf Cakes

What you will need:

Batter:
- 3 eggs
- 1 cup sugar
- 1-1/2 cups all purpose flour
- 1 cup plain yogurt
- 1/2 cup vegetable oil
- 2 TBSP grated lemon zest
- 2 TBSP lemon juice
- 1 cup freeze dried blueberries
- 2 tsp baking powder
- 1 tsp Himalayan pink salt, fine grind

Icing:
- 1 cup confectioners sugar
- 2 TBSP lemon juice

Instructions:

1. Preheat oven to 350F.

2. Grease mini loaves pan or 9 in (22cm) x 4 in (10cm) bread loaf pan.

3. Combine all ingredients just until moistened.

4. Bake mini loaves for 40 minutes or until golden brown and set in the middle.

5. Mix together icing ingredients. Drizzle icing over cooled loaves.

Yield: This recipe makes 12 mini loaf cakes.

Lime Raspberry Loaf Cake

What you will need:

Batter:
- 3 eggs
- 1 cup sugar
- 1-1/2 cups all purpose flour
- 1 cup plain yogurt
- 1/2 cup vegetable oil
- 2 TBSP grated lime zest
- 2 TBSP lime juice
- 1 cup freeze dried raspberries
- 2 tsp baking powder
- 1 tsp Himalayan pink salt, fine grind

Icing:
- 1 cup confectioners sugar
- 2 TBSP lime juice

Instructions:

1. Preheat oven to 350F.

2. Grease 8 in (20cm) x 4 in (10cm) bread loaf pan.

3. Combine all ingredients just until moistened.

4. Bake for 65 minutes, or until golden brown and set in the middle.

5. Mix together confectioners icing ingredients. Drizzle icing over cooled loaf cake.

Yield: This recipe makes one loaf cake.

Orange Cardamom Mini Muffins

What you will need:

Batter:
- 3 eggs
- 1 cups sugar
- 1-1/2 cups all purpose flour
- 1 cup plain yogurt
- 1/2 cup vegetable oil
- 2 TBSP grated orange zest
- 1/4 cup orange juice
- 2 tsps cardamom, ground
- 2 tsp baking powder
- 1 tsp Himalayan pink salt, fine grind

Icing:
- 1 cup confectioners sugar
- 2 TBSP orange juice
- 2 TBSP orange zest
- 1/2 tsp cardamom, ground
- 1/2 tsp vanilla extract

Instructions:

1. Preheat oven to 350F.

2. Grease mini muffin pans.

3. Combine all ingredients just until moistened.

4. Bake for 20 minutes.

5. Mix together icing ingredients. Drizzle icing over cooled mini muffins.

Yield: This recipe makes 24 mini muffins.

Note: each recipe can be made as full-sized loaf cake, mini loaf cakes or mini muffins. Adjust cooking times accordingly.

Sweet Pickled Relish

What you will need:

- 2 cups 1/4 in (6cm) diced English cucumber
- 4 oz 1/4 in (6cm) diced red bell pepper
- 1 tsp mustard seed
- 1 tsp onion powder
- 1 tsp garlic powder
- 3 TBSP sugar
- 1 cup apple cider vinegar
- 2 cups water
- 1 tsp Himalayan pink salt, fine grind
- (2) 16 oz (454g) Mason jars

Instructions:

1. Sterilize jars.

2. Evenly distribute cucumbers and peppers between the two jars.

3. Mix together remaining ingredients in pot on stove. Heat, stirring until salt and sugar are dissolved.

4. Pour liquid evenly over both jars.

Moroccan Pickled Carrots

What you will need:

- 12 oz peeled carrots cut into 1/2 in (12cm) sticks
- 1 tsp minced garlic
- 1/2 tsp minced jalapeno pepper
- 1 tsp ground cumin
- 1 cup white vinegar
- 2 cups water
- 1 tsp Himalayan pink salt, fine gring
- 2 TBSP coarsely chopped cilantro
- (2) 16 oz (454g) Mason jars

Instructions:

1. Sterilize jars.

2. Pack carrots tightly in jars vertically.

3. Mix together the garlic, pepper, cumin, vinegar, water, salt and cilantro in pot on stove. Heat, stirring until salt is dissolved.

4. Pour liquid evenly over both jars.

Asian Pickled Green Beans

What you will need:

- 12 oz trimmed green beans
- 1 tsp grated ginger
- 1 tsp prepared horseradish
- 1 cup rice wine vinegar
- 2 cups water
- 1 tsp Himalayan pink salt, fine grind
- a few drops pure (light) sesame oil
- (2) 16 oz (454g) Mason jars

Instructions:

1. Sterilize jars.

2. Pack beans tightly in jars vertically.

3. Mix together ginger, horseradish, vinegar, water, salt, and sesame oil in pot on stove. Heat, stirring until salt is dissolved.

4. Pour liquid evenly over both jars.

PICKLES

Refrigerator pickles are super easy to make. They don't last as long as traditional canned goods, but they don't take as long to make, either. As long as you keep them in the refrigerator, they will last up to one month.

I discovered both the Moroccan and Asian flavor profiles while living in Israel. You can add any crunchy vegetable to any of these pickling liquids, including traditional cucumber pickles! Asparagus, cauliflower, radishes and turnips also make wonderful refrigerator pickles. Pickles are a fantastic snack - a great crunch with bold flavors. And they are always a great accompaniment to sandwiches or a table spread of tapas and appetizers.

I love to add this relish to tuna salad or potato salad for a zing. It is one of my favorite go-to lunch recipes when I'm working and don't have time to cook.

TRUFFLES

Chocolate truffles are one of the most deceptively easy treats I know how to make. Mix up the flavorings for an assorted gift, too.

What you will need:

- 1 pastry box 5.5 in (14cm) x 2.75 in (7cm) x 1.75 in (4cm) with six 1 inch (25cm) paper cup liners
- 1 cup heavy cream
- 1 lb semi-sweet chocolate chips
- 1 tsp vanilla extract
- 8 oz melting chocolate for dipping

Option 1:
Decorate with assorted sprinkles, candies and sugars.

Option 2:
Instead of melted chocolate coating, roll truffles in cocoa powder for a dusted chocolate look.

Yield: This recipe makes one dozen (12) truffles.

Instructions:

1. Heat the heavy cream over medium heat until hot but not boiling.

2. Pour the hot cream over the chocolate chips and slowly stir until melted and smooth.

3. Allow melted chocolate to cool in refrigerator for 30 minutes.

4. Scoop out the stiffened chocolate ganache with a tablespoon and roll into balls in your hands (each one should be approx. 1 inch or 2.5cm diameter). Set onto parchment paper.

5. Melt dipping chocolate.

6. Dip ganache balls (truffle centers) into the melted chocolate.

Note: You may wish to use a long wooden skewer poked into the truffle to dip it. Place the dipped truffle back onto parchment paper to cool and set.

7. Decorate truffles with sprinkles, candies or sugars before the chocolate sets.

8. Assemble your truffles in pastry boxes.

CHEESE LOG

I have been making homemade cheese dips and cheese logs for as long as I can remember. Once you understand the basic ratio, you can add whatever flavors strike your fancy. But you can't go wrong with a citrus-herb-garlic combination!

What you will need:

- 8 oz block of cream cheese, room temperature
- 8 oz sharp white cheddar cheese, grated
- 1 clove garlic, finely minced
- 2 TBSP chives, finely chopped
- 2 TBSP parsley, finely chopped
- juice and zest of 1 lemon
- pinch of cayenne pepper
- freshly ground pepper to taste
- 1/2 cup roasted, salted pistachios, finely chopped

Note: If desired you can replace traditional cream cheese with goat cheese or probiotic cashew cheese (pg 20).

Yield: This recipe makes two 6 in (15cm) logs.

Instructions:

1. Mix the cream cheese, cheddar cheese, garlic, chives, parsely, lemon zest and juice, cayenne, and pepper together in a bowl until thoroughly combined.

2. Lay a large piece of plastic wrap on a work surface and put the cheese mixture on top. Use the plastic wrap to form it into a 12 in (30cm) log. Refrigerate until firm, about 1 hour.

3. Finely chop pistachios and spread them on a flat work surface covered in plastic wrap. Unwrap the cheese log; cut into two equal pieces and roll one at a time in the pistachios until completely coated. Rewrap in clean plastic wrap and refrigerate up to one day.

As a gift, wrap in butcher paper and tie with ribbon or put cheese log in a pastry box and tie with ribbon. Serve with an assortment of crackers and crunchy crudite.

CHEESE CRACKERS

If you love cheese crackers, you will LOVE homemade cheese crackers. This is a basic recipe - add spices or blend different cheeses for variety. Or experiment with alternative flours for a gluten-free gift!

What you will need:

- 8 oz sharp cheddar cheese
- 1/4 cup cold, salted butter
- 1 cup flour
- 1 tsp salt
- 1 tsp smoked paprika
- 1 - 3 tsp cold water

Option 1:
Add 1/2 tsp each of onion powder and garlic powder

Option 2:
Mix 3 parts cheddar to 1 part parmesan for a stronger cheese flavor.

Option 3:
Mix 1 part cheddar, 1 part pepper jack for a spicier flavor.

Option 4:
Add 2 tsp finely chopped fresh herbs (like thyme, oregano, rosemary or lemon zest) for an aromatic flavor.

Instructions:

1. Grate the cheese and cube the butter.

2. Place all ingredients except water in the food processor and pulse to combine. Run on low while you add the water, one tsp at a time. When the mixture binds and forms a ball, stop adding water and remove from processor. The heat and humidity will greatly impact the amount of water you many need to add, but I was good after 2 tsps.

3. Wrap dough in plastic wrap and refrigerate for at least one hour.

4. Preheat oven to 400 F.

5. Cut dough in half, roll out on a floured surface to a very thin sheet (approx 1/8" or 3cm) and transfer to a lined cookie sheet.

Note: Silicone liners are great, but if you don't have them, parchment paper works well, too.

6. Score with a pastry wheel or gently roll a knife or pizza cutter over the surface to get your score lines. Prick the center of each square with a fork.

7. Bake for 15 minutes for chewy crackers, or up to 17 minutes for crispier crackers. The chewy ones taste cheesier but the crispier ones have a great snap. Try both!

Yield: This recipe makes 24 two inch (5cm) crackers.

QUINOA CRACKERS

Whether you are vegan, gluten-free or not, you probably have friends that are. What a better way to support their journey than with a delicious treat!

What you will need:

- 1 cup cooked and cooled quinoa
- 1/3 cup chia seeds
- 1 cup water
- 1/2 cup hemp seeds
- 1/4 cup sesame seeds
- 1 tsp smoked paprika
- 1 TBSP nutritional yeast
- Himalayan pink salt and freshly ground black pepper to taste

Yield: This recipe makes 24 three inch (7cm) crackers.

Instructions:

1. Preheat oven to 350 F degrees.

2. Soak chia seeds in the water for 5 minutes. Do not drain.

3. Mix all ingredients together in large bowl.

4. Line baking sheet with parchment paper or silicone liner.

5. Spread the mixture evenly over baking sheet, spreading it to 1/4" (6cm) thin, trying to smooth the edges into a rectangle.

6. Bake for 30 minutes.

7. Cut crackers into squares.

8. Flip each one over with a spatula.

9. Bake for an additional 30 minute.

PROBIOTIC CASHEW CHEESE

Probiotic vegan cashew cream cheese is a surprisingly easy, delicious and healthy ingredient that is yummy on its own and can be substituted in many recipes that call for traditional cream cheese. It is super simple to make, and can be flavored in dozens of ways. This recipe yields 2 cups of cashew cheese. Based on a 1 TBSP serving, you will get 16 servings from this recipe.

What you will need:

- 2 cups cashews
- 2 TBSP non-dairy plain, unsweetened yogurt
- 1 tsp Himalayan pink salt, fine grind

Instructions:

1. Soak the cashews overnight in water.

Note: In a hurry? Soak the cashews in boiling hot water from the kettle for an hour instead.

2. Drain the cashews. Add to blender or food processor with the yogurt and salt. Blend until smooth.

3. Transfer to a clean container and cover. Allow to sit at room temperature for 24 - 48 hours. Use a clean utensil to taste the mixture at 24 hours; add more salt if needed. Allow culture to sit another 12 - 24 hours if more tang is desired.

4. Store in refrigerator for up to 1 week.

You can add any number of flavors to this cream cheese. It can be used to schmear on any baked goods; it can replace cream cheese in recipes like jalapeno poppers, and it makes a great dip for pretzels or crudite, too!

I love adding scallions and chives for a classic savory flavor. Or chopped smoked salmon and fresh dill for a brunch schmear. Chopped sundried tomatoes folded in make a beautiful and delicious spread. Honey and cinnamon swirled in makes a great sweet spread, too! I love this on sprouted grain toast for breakfast.

COCOA MIX

Homemade hot cocoa is comfort in a cup. For a more graphic display, layer the ingredients in the jars instead of mixing together.

What you will need:

- 7 cups non-fat dry milk
- 2 cups cocoa powder
- 2 cups confectioners sugar

Note: This recipe yields 12 cups before adding any of the options below.

Each optional flavoring is for 1/3 of the full recipe, or 4 cups of cocoa mix.

Option 1:
- 1 cup mini marshmallows
- 1 cup mini chocolate chips

Option 2:
- 2 TBSP ground cinnamon
- 1/2 tsp cayenne pepper

Option 3:
- 1/2 cup hard peppermint candies, crushed

Option 4:
- 1/2 cup caramel hard candies, crushed
- 1/2 tsp Himalayan pink salt, fine grind

Option 5:
- 1/2 cup instant coffee

Instructions:

1. Mix milk powder, cocoa powder and sugar together until well combined.

2. If flavoring with any of the listed options, add to the mix now.

3. Add cocoa mix to sealable jars.

4. Make instruction card.

Card:

Fill 1/3 to 1/2 of a mug with cocoa mix. Add hot water or milk and stir until mix is dissolved.

FLAVORED SUGARS

Flavored sugars are a great alternative to syrup on pancakes or toast; it can be used as a unique sweetener for cocoa or tea; to rim cocktail glasses, or having fun when rolling sugar cookies and shortbread. I separated the recipes into three categories based on the moisture content of the flavors.

Make a collection of flavored sugars for a thematic gift set. 3 oz (88ml) spice jars are well suited for 2 in (5cm) by 4 in (10cm) address labels. I printed these from online templates.

Yield: Each batch fills one spice jar.

Dried Fruit Sugars

What you will need:

- 1/2 cup sugar
- 1 cup freeze dried strawberries, pineapple, blueberries, mango or raspberries
- 3 oz (88ml) spice jars

Note: Recipe is for one flavor per batch.

Instructions:

1. Pulverize sugar and flavor in food processor.

2. Store in airtight container.

Dried Flower or Spice Sugars

What you will need:

- 1 cup sugar
- 1 tsp (5ml) dried lavender buds or rose petals or
- 1 - 2 tsps ground ginger, cardamon, chile powder, cinnamon or star anise
- 3 oz (88ml) spice jars

Note: Recipe is for one spice per batch.

Instructions:

1. Pulverize sugar and flavor in food processor.

2. Store in airtight container.

Citrus Zest Sugars

What you will need:

- 1 cup sugar
- zest of one lemon, lime, orange or grapefruit (zested right over the sugar for extra flavor)
- 3 oz (88ml) spice jars

Note: Recipe is for one zest per batch.

Zest dries out in sugar so there is no need to sieve out.

Instructions:

1. Mix ingredients together.

2. Store in airtight container.

PEACH CHUTNEY

Chutney is a sweet, tangy and spicy fruit preserve that can be made with many fruits including peach, pineapple, mango or apple. Spread it on grilled cheese or deli sandwiches. Add a dollop to steamed rice or roasted potatoes. Brush it on grilled fish or pork just before taking off the heat.

What you will need:

- 6 cups diced peaches, peeled and diced 1/2 in (13cm)
- 1-1/2 cups red onion, finely chopped 1/4 in (6cm)
- 2 TBSP fresh ginger root, peeled and grated
- 1-1/2 cups brown sugar
- 1 cup apple cider vinegar
- 1-1/2 tsp cayenne pepper
- 1-1/2 tsp cardamom, ground
- 1-1/2 tsp Himalayn pink salt, fine grind
- zest and juice of one lime

Instructions:

1. Add everything, except lime zest and juice, to a medium saucepan.

2. Bring to a simmer and cook uncovered on low heat for one hour. Allow to cool completely. Chutney thickens as it cools.

3. Once cooled, add lime zest and juice.

4. Store in airtight containers in refrigerator for up to one month.

Mason jars and glass jars with metal flip lids work very well for chutney gifts.

Yield: This recipe makes four 8 oz jars of chutney.

MARLENE

Drawstring Bag

A drawstring bag is an elegant way to present a gift. Fill it with yarn, fabric, or clothing and let the gifts peek through these pretty lace motifs. Or line it and give this as a stand-alone gift.

What you will need:

- 400 yds (360m) #2 sport weight yarn
- F/5 (3.75mm) crochet hook
- 1/2 yd (.44m) of cotton fabric for lining
- Yarn needle
- Sewing needle
- Scissors

Shown in:
Be So Fresh Yarn; 100% linen; 300 yds (274m) per 3.5oz (100g); color Foam

Gauge:
Each motif is 3 in (7cm) square after blocking.

Finished Size:
24 in (61cm) circumference

Stitch Guide:
See glossary for chain, single crochet, slip stitch, double crochet, treble crochet, foundation oval, 2-Treble Crochet Cluster and 3-Treble Crochet Cluster.

Instructions:

First Motif:

Ch5, slst to 5th ch from hook to join in ring.

Round 1: Ch4 (counts as dc, ch1), (dc in ring, ch1)x11, slst to 3rd of beg ch to join. — 12 dcs

Round 2: Slst into first ch1 sp, ch4 (counts as tr), 2-tr cl in same st, *ch5, 3-tr cl in next ch1 sp. Rep from * around, ch2, dc in top of ch4 at beg of round to join (ch2 and dc counts as last ch5 sp). — 12 ch5 sps

Round 3: Ch1, sc in same sp, *ch1, in next ch5 sp work [(dc, ch1)x3, tr, (ch1, dc)x2], ch1, sc in next ch5 sp, ch5, sc in next ch5 sp. Rep from * around, replace last sc with slst to first sc at beg of round to join. Fasten off. — 4 corners and 4 ch5 sps

Second & Third Motifs (one - side joining):

Rounds 1 - 2: Rep rounds 1 - 2 of first motif.

Round 3: Ch1, sc in same sp, ch1, in next ch5 sp work [(dc, ch1)x3, tr, (ch1, dc)x3], ch1, sc in next ch5 sp, ch5, sc in next ch5 sp. In next ch5 sp work [(dc, ch1)x3, tr, (slst in adjacent motif's ch1 sp, dc)x3, ch1, sc in next ch5 sp, ch2, slst in adjacent

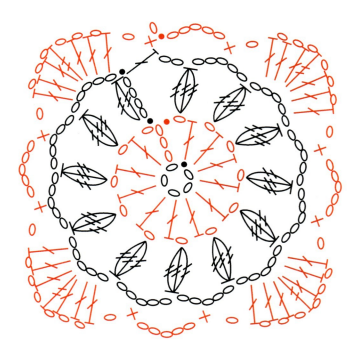

motif's ch5 sp, ch2, sc in next ch5 sp, ch1, in next ch5 sp work [(dc, slst in adjacent motif's ch1 sp)x3, tr, (ch1, dc)x3], ch1, sc in next ch5 sp, ch5, sc in next ch5 sp, ch1, in next ch5 sp work [(dc, ch1)x3, tr, (ch1, dc)x3], ch1, sc in next ch5 sp, ch5, slst to first st at beg of round to join. Fasten off. — 4 corners and 4 ch5 sps

Fourth Motif (two - side joining):

Rounds 1 - 2: Rep rounds 1 - 2 of first motif.

Round 3: Ch1, sc in same sp, ch1, in next ch5 sp work [(dc, ch1)x3, tr, (ch1, dc)x3], ch1, sc in next ch5 sp, ch5, sc in next ch5 sp, ch1. In next ch5 sp work [(dc, ch1)x3, tr, (slst in adjacent motif's ch1 sp, dc)x3], *ch1, sc in next ch5 sp, ch2, slst[25] in adjacent motif's ch5 sp, ch2, sc in next ch5 sp, ch1, in next ch5 sp work [(dc, slst in adjacent motif's ch1 sp) x3, tr, (ch1, dc)x3], ch1, sc in next ch5 sp, ch5, sc in next ch5 sp, ch1, in next ch5 sp work [(dc, ch1)x3, tr, (ch1, dc) x3]. Rep from * once more, ch1, sc in next ch5 sp, ch5, sls to first st at beg of round to join.
Fasten off. — 4 corners and 4 ch5 sps

Joining Front and Back together:

Back:
Round 1: Join with slst to

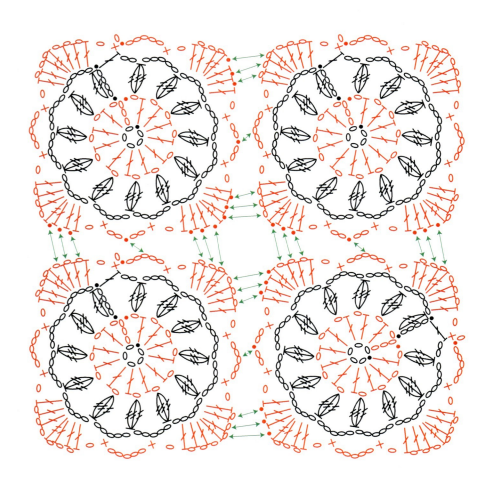

any 2nd ch1 sp in corner shell, ch1, *sc in same sp, ch7, skip corner ch1 sp, sc in next ch1 sp, ch7, sc in next ch5 sp, ch7, skip next 2 ch1 sps, sc in next ch1 sp, skip next ch1 sp on current motif and next motif, sc in next ch1 sp, ch7, sc in next ch5 sp, skip next two ch1 sps, sc in next ch1 sp, ch7, skip next ch1 sp on current motif and next motif, sc in next ch1 sp, ch7, sc in next ch5 sp, ch7, skip next two ch1 sps, sc in next ch1 sp, ch7. Rep from * around. Slst to top of first st at beg of round to join. -- 40 ch7 sps

Front: Rep round 1 for back, except on 3 sides replace ch7 with ch7 join to adjacent ch7 sps on back.

Note: Three sides of front and back are joined and the exposed top of front and back will now be crocheted into as a round.

Band:

Round 1: Work 9sc in ea ch7 sp around. Slst to first st at beg of round to join. -- 180 sts

Round 2: Slst in ea of next 2 sts, ch2, 1dc in ea of the 5 center sts in the 9sc of previous round, *ch1, skip 4 sts, 1dc in ea of next 5 sts. Rep from * around, slst to top of first st at beg of round to join. -- 100 dcs, 20 ch1 sps

Round 3: Ch1, sc in ea st and ch1 sp around, slst to top of first st at beg of round to join. -- 120 sts

Round 4: Ch1, sc in ea st around, slst to top of first st at beg of round to join. -- 120 sts

Round 5: Ch2, 1dc in ea st around, slst to top of first st at beg of round to join. -- 120 sts

Round 6: Rep round 4.

Round 7: Slst in ea st around. Fasten off.

Ties (make 2):

Ch150. Fasten off.

Tassels (make 4):

Cut 2 pieces of yarn, 12 in (30cm) each, set aside. Wrap yarn around 3 in (8cm) piece of cardboard 30 times, cut on one side creating 1 bundle of 30 strands. Place bundle evenly centered on one of the 12 in (30cm) pieces of yarn, tie bundle into place (assure strands are even). Fold bundle so that strands are even, tie second 12 in (30cm) piece of yarn around bundle, 0.5 in (1.25cm) below first knot. Trim bundle ends even. Holding two strands of yarn together, join to center front. Sew to end of each chain tie with a square knot. Weave in ends.

Finishing:

Weave in loose ends. Hand wash, block to finished measurements and allow to dry.

Lining (optional):

Cut 2 pieces of fabric 25 in (63cm) square and pin right sides together and sew 1/2 in (13cm) seam along 3 sides. Press seam open with iron. Insert bag inside lining with right sides facing (you should be looking at wrong side of lining facing you). Sew along top leaving a 4 in (10cm) opening for turning. Turn right side out and push lining into bag. Your bag should be right side facing with the lining showing inside the bag (wrong sides of bag and fabric facing). Press seam with iron. Hand stitch opening closed.

Note: If lining, don't add the chain and tassels until the sewing is complete.

HOPE
Case

A lace bag is an elegant way to present a gift. Fill it with yarn, reading glasses, sunglasses, notions, or rolled up fabric or clothing. Or line it and give this as a stand-alone gift.

What you will need:

- 80 yds (73m) #2 sport weight yarn
- F/5 (3.75mm) crochet hook
- Yarn needle
- Scissors
- 1/4 yd (.22m) fabric (optional)
- Sewing needle

Shown in:
Be So Fresh Yarn; 100% linen yarn; 300 yds (274m) per 3.5oz (100g); color Sand Dollar

Gauge:
2 pattern repeats = 4 in (10cm) square

Finished Size:
4.5 in (11cm) wide x 6 in (15cm) tall

Stitch Guide:
See glossary for chain, single crochet, double crochet, foundation oval, and half double crochet.

Instructions:

Body:

Set up row: *Ch4, tr in 4th ch from hook. Rep from * 4 more times. -- 5 foundation ovals

Round 1: Ch1, sc in same st, (7dc in space of next foundation oval, sc in space of next foundation oval) x2, in next foundation oval work (7dc, sc, 7dc). At this point, turn your work 180 degrees so you can work into the opposite side of the foundation ovals. *Sc in space of next foundation oval (working into the opposite side of the foundation ovals), 7dc in next foundation oval. Rep from * once more, slst to first sc at beg of round to join. — 6 7dc shells

Note: You will be working around the entire perimeter of the foundation oval row and working in the round for the remainder of this project.

Round 2: Slst into ea of next 2 dcs, ch1, sc in same st, *ch5, skip next 3 sts, sc in next st. Rep from * around, on last rep, replace last ch5 sp with ch2, dc in first st at beg of round to join. — 12 ch5 sps

Round 3: Ch1, sc in same ch5 sp, *ch5, sc in next ch5 sp. Rep from * around, replace last ch5 sp with ch2, dc in first st at beg of round to join. — 6 ch5 sps

Round 4: rep round 3

Round 5: Ch1, sc in same st, 7dc in next ch5 sp, sc in next ch5 sp. Rep from * around, replace last sc with slst to first sc at beg of round to join. — 6 7dc shells

Rounds 6 - 13: Rep rounds 2 - 5 two more times.

Handles:

Round 1: Slst into ea of next 2 sts, ch1, 1sc in ea of next 5 sts, ch1, skip 3 sts, 1sc in ea of next 5 sts. Rep from * around, ch1, slst to first st at beg of round to join. — 30 scs, 6 ch1 sps

Round 2: Ch1, 1sc in ea of next 5 sts, 1sc in next ch1 sp. Rep from * around, slst to first st at beg of round to join. — 36 sts

Round 3: Ch1, sc in ea st around, slst to first st at beg of round to join. — 36 sts

Rounds 4 - 5: Rep round 3.

Round 6: Ch1, sc in ea of next 4 sts, slst in ea of next 10 sts, sc in ea of next 8 sts, slst in ea of next 10 sts, sc in ea of next 4 sts, slst to first st at beg of round to join.

Round 7: Ch1, sc in ea of next 4 sts, ch18, skip next 10 slsts, sc in ea of next 8 sts, ch18, skip next 10 slsts, sc in ea of next 4 sts, slst to first st at beg of round to join.

Round 8: Ch1, sc in ea of next 4 sts, 1sc in ea of next 18 chs, sc in ea of next 8 sts, 1sc in ea of next 18 chs, sc in ea of next 4 sts, slst to first st at beg of round to join.

Round 9: Ch1, sc in ea st around, slst to first st at beg of round to join.

Rounds 10 - 11: Rep round 9.

Round 12: Slst around. Fasten off.

Finishing:

Weave in loose ends. Hand wash, block to finished measurements and allow to dry.

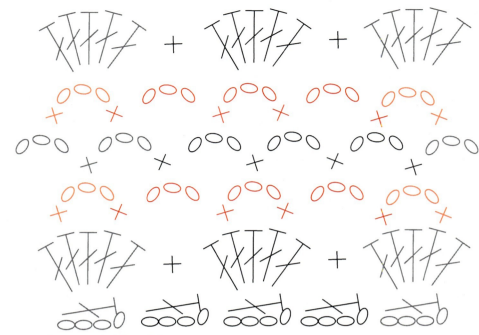

Lining (optional):

Cut 2 pieces of fabric 5.5 in (14cm) square. Pin right sides together and sew 1/2 in (13cm) seam along 3 sides. Press seam open with iron. Insert bag inside lining with right sides facing (you should be looking at wrong side of lining facing you). Sew along top leaving a 4 in (10cm) opening for turning. Turn right side out and push lining into bag. Your bag should be right side facing with the lining showing inside the bag (wrong sides of bag and fabric facing). Press seam with iron. Hand stitch opening closed.

ABIGAIL
Market Tote

This bag starts with a traditional granny square base and the starburst, chevron pattern is accentuated with contrasting stripes. Choose your loved one's signature colors for a utilitarian market bag that brings a smile to their face every single day.

What you will need:

- 120 yds (110m) #2 sport weight yarn
- G/6 (4mm) crochet hook
- Yarn needle
- Scissors

Shown in:
Be So Serene Yarn; 100% organic cotton; 315 yds (288m) per 4oz (113g); color A Lovable and color B Bare

Stitch Guide:

See glossary for chain, slip stitch, single crochet, double crochet and 4-dc cluster.

Gauge:

1 rep / 5 rows = 4 in (10cm) in pattern

Finished Size:

4 in (10cm) square base, 7 in (18cm) wide x 9 in (23cm) tall, 7 in (18cm) handle drop

Instructions:

Base:

With color A, ch5, slst to 5th ch from hook to form ring.

Round 1: Ch3 (counts as dc), dc in ring, *ch1, 2dc in ring. Rep from * 6 more times, sc to top of first st at beg of round to join. Last sc counts as ch1 sp. -- 16 dcs, 8 ch1 sps

Round 2: With color B, join with slst in same sp as last st, ch3 (counts as dc), dc in same sp, *ch2, 2dc in next ch1 sp, ch2, (2dc, ch2, 2dc) in next ch1 sp. Rep from * around, ch2, 2dc in next ch1 sp, ch2, 2dc in first ch1 sp, ch1, sc to top of first st at beg of round to join. Last (ch1, sc) counts as a ch2 sp. -- 24 dcs, 12 ch2 sps

Note: Alternate between the two colors. All even numbered rows are color B and all odd numbered rows are color A. Carry the yarns instead of cutting after each round.

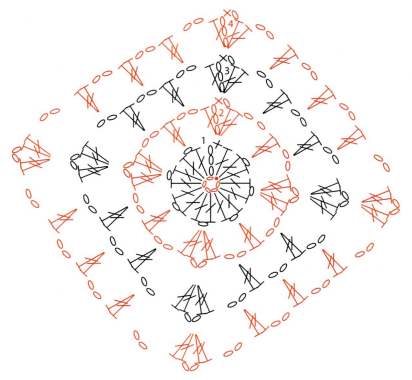

Handles:

Round 14: Ch1, sc in same sp, (1sc in ea st and ch to center of next shell's ch2 sp (18 scs), ch54, sc in center ch2 of next shell, 1sc in ea st and ch to center of next shell's ch2 sp (18 scs), ch54, slst to first st at beg of round to join. -- 36 scs, 108 chs

Round 15: Ch1, sc in ea st and ch around. -- 144 scs

Round 16: Slst in ea st around. Fasten off.

Finishing:

Weave in loose ends. Hand wash, block to finished measurements and allow to dry.

Round 3: With color A, ch3 (counts as dc), dc in same sp, *(ch2, 2dc in next ch2 sp)x2, ch2, (2dc, ch2, 2dc) in next ch2 sp. Rep from * around, (ch2, 2dc in next ch2 sp)x2, ch2, 2dc in first ch1 sp, ch1, sc in top of first st at beg of round to join. -- 32 dcs, 16 ch2 sps

Round 4: With color B, ch3 (counts as dc), dc in same sp, *(ch2, 2dc in next ch2 sp)x3, ch2, (2dc, ch3, 2dc) in next ch2 sp. Rep from * around, (ch2, 2dc in next ch2 sp)x3, ch2, 2dc in first ch1 sp, ch1, sc to top of first st at beg of round to join. -- 40 dcs, 20 ch2 sps

Sides:

Rounds 5 - 13: Ch3 (counts as dc), dc in same sp, *ch2, 2dc in next ch2 sp, ch2, dc4tog over next 2 ch2 sps, ch2, 2dc in next ch2 sp, ch2, **(2dc, ch2, 2dc) in next ch2 sp. Rep from * around, rep from * to ** once more, dc in first ch1 sp, ch1, sc to top of first st at beg of round to join. -- 24 dcs, 4 dc4tog, 20 ch2 sps

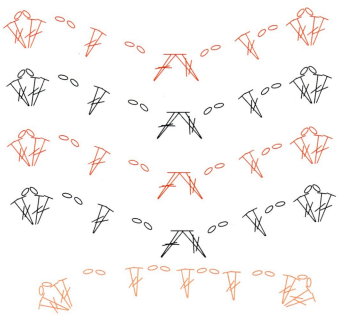

JENNIFER

Crochet Motif Bowl

Surprise a friend with a stylish and completely hardened yarn bowl! Filling it with items in contrasting colors really makes the lacework pop. Adding gold leaf to the rim would elevate the elegance or try spray painting the entire bowl with metallic paint.

What you will need:

- 300 yds (274m) #1 fingering weight yarn
- G/6 (4mm) crochet hook
- Yarn needle
- Scissors
- Smooth-On Smooth-Cast 325 Liquid Plastic
- Latex gloves
- Disposable bowl and stir stick
- Balloon or silcone mold, approx. 8 - 10 in (20-25cm) diameter

Shown in:
Be So Fine Yarn; 100% bamboo; 650 yds (594m) per 4oz (113g); color Lilac Memories

Gauge:
Each motif is 4 in (10cm) square after blocking.

Finished Size:
Bowl is 4 in (10cm) tall with 10 in (25cm) diameter

Stitch Guide:
See glossary for chain, single crochet, double crochet, slst, ch5 join and picot join.

Instructions:

First Motif:

Ch5, slst to 5th ch from hook to form ring.

Round 1: Ch3 (counts as dc), dc in ring, *ch3, 2dc in ring. Rep from * two more times, ch3, slst to top of first st at beg of round to join. -- 8 dcs, 4 ch3 sps

Round 2: Ch1, sc in same st, *ch5, sc in next st, ch5, sc in next ch3 sp, ch5, sc in next st. Rep from * around, except on last rep replace last sc with slst to top of first st at beg of round to join. -- 12 ch5 sps

Round 3: Slst into next ch5 sp, ch3 (counts as dc), work 7dc in same sp, *sc in next ch5 sp, ch5, sc in next ch5 sp, 8dc in next ch5 sp. Rep from * around, sc in next ch5, sp, ch5, sc in next ch5 sp, slst to top of first st at beg of round to join. -- 4 8dc corners, 4 ch5 sps

Round 4: Ch4 (counts as dc, ch1), (dc, ch1)x2, dc, ch5, (dc, ch1)x3, dc, *ch2,

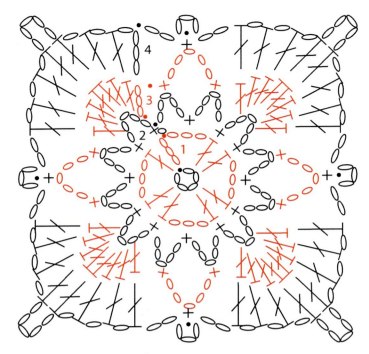

sc in next ch5 sp, ch3, slst to 3rd ch from hook (picot made), ch2, (dc in next st, ch1)x3, dc, ch5, (dc, ch1)3, dc in next st. Rep from * around, ch2, sc in next ch5 sp, ch3 picot, ch2, slst to top of first st at beg of round to join. Fasten off. -- 4 ch5 corners, 4 ch3 picots

Second Motif (one-side joining):

Rounds 1 - 3: Rep rounds 1 - 3 of first motif.

Round 4: Rep round 4 of first motif except replace ch5 with ch5 join and replace picot with picot join along one side.

Two-sided joining motif:

Rounds 1 - 3: Rep rounds 1 - 3 of first motif.

Round 4: Rep round 4 of first motif except replace ch5 with ch5 join and replace picot with picot join along two sides.

Three-sided joining motif:

Rounds 1 - 3: Rep rounds 1 - 3 of first motif.

Round 4: Rep round 4 of first motif except replace ch5 with ch5 join and replace picot with picot join along three sides.

Finishing:

Weave in loose ends. Saturate in solution per manufacturer's instructions, squeeze out the excess solution, block to bowl shape and allow to dry.

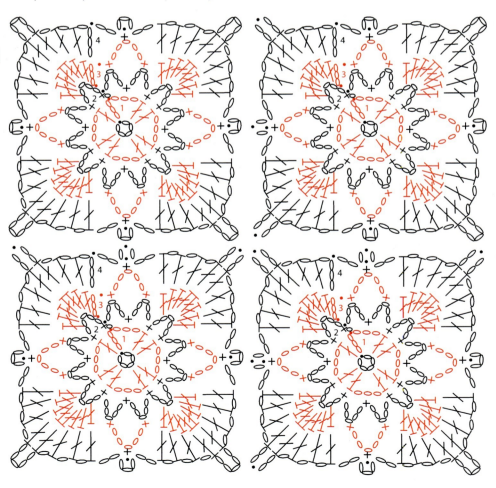

BELLE
Lace Edged Napkin

A bandana is an iconic piece of fabric. Already hemmed and fine enough to easily pierce with a small crochet hook, it provides you a fantastic base for crocheting on fabric. You can elevate a bandana into a fancy headscarf, a liner for a breadbasket or a wrap for a special homemade cake.

What you will need:

- 70 yds (64m) #1 fingering weight yarn
- 1.0mm crochet hook
- B/1 (2.25mm) crochet hook
- 22 in (56cm) cotton bandana
- Yarn needle

Shown in:
Be So Fine Yarn; 100% bamboo; 650 yds (594m) per 4oz (113g); color Chantilly Lace

Gauge:
Not critical for this project. Edging repeat is 1/2 in (13cm) wide x 1/2 in (13cm) tall

Finished Size:
23 in (58cm) square bandana

Special Stitch Instructions:
See Glossary for slst, chain, single crochet, double crochet

Instructions:

Note: The smaller crochet hook is sharp enough to pierce this fabric directly for crocheting right onto the fabric.

Round 1: With smaller crochet hook, join with slst to any corner of fabric. Ch1, sc in same spot, ch5, sc in same corner. *ch5, sc 1 in (2.5cm) away from the last st. Rep from * across to next corner, ch5, sc in same sp as last sc. Rep from * for each side of fabric. Slst to first st at beg of round to join. -- 4 ch5 corners, 88 ch5 sps along sides

Round 2: With larger crochet hook, work (sc, ch2, 3dc, ch3, 3dc, ch2, sc) in ea ch5 sp around. slst to first st at beg of round to join. Fasten off.

Finishing:
Weave in loose ends. Hand wash, block to finished measurements and allow to dry.

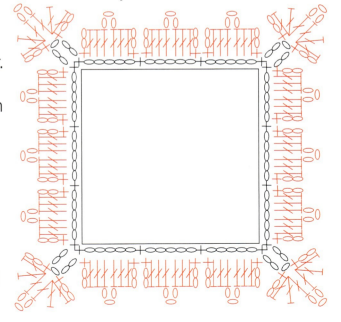

CAMI
Skinny Scarf

If you are new to Tunisian double crochet, a narrow row is a great introduction to this simple technique. The openwork makes a beautiful scarf which can also be worn as a sash belt or as a headband.

What you will need:

- 247 yds (225m) #4 worsted weight yarn
- J/10 (6mm) crochet hook
- Yarn needle
- Scissors

Shown in:
Be So Bold Yarn; 51% organic cotton, 49% bamboo; 247 yds (225m) per 4oz (113g); color Serengeti Sunrise

Note: Tunisian crochet hook is not required for this project.

Gauge:
14 sts / 4 rows = 4 in (10cm) in blocked stitch pattern

Finished Size:
2 in (5cm) wide x 72 in (183cm) long

Special Stitch Instructions:
See Glossary for Tunisian double crochet.

Instructions:

Row 1: Ch9, yo, insert hook in 4th ch from hook, yo, pull through 2 loops. Rep from * five more times. You should have 7 loops on crochet hook.
Return: yo, pull through 1 loop, *yo, pull through 2 loops. Rep from * across.

Row 2: Ch3, *yo, insert hook in vertical bar in next st, yo, pull through 2 loops. Rep from * across. You should have 7 loops on crochet hook.
Return: yo, pull through 1 loop, *yo, pull through 2 loops. Rep from * across.

Rows 3 - 69: rep row 2

Row 70: Loosely slst in ea vertical bar across. Fasten off.

Finishing:

Weave in loose ends. Hand wash, block to finished measurements and allow to dry.

CELESTE
Earrings

Earrings are a great excuse for going all out with texture and sparkle! The simplicity of the stitches allows the yarn to shine. These are simple to whip up for last minute gifts. Thinner yarn and a smaller hook will result in smaller earrings.

What you will need:

- 50 yds (46)m #4 worsted weight yarn (or equivalent when held together)
- G/6 (4mm) crochet hook
- (2) jump rings
- (2) french hooks
- Yarn needle
- Scissors
- (2) pairs of chain nose or bent nose pliers

Shown in:
Be So Dazzling Yarn; 100% polyester; 100 yds (45m) per 1 oz (25gm) spool; color Silver

Be So Sporty BLING Yarn; 90% bamboo, 10% silver; 300 yds (274m) per 4oz (113gm); color Mermaid 01

Gauge:
5 sts / 5 rows = 1 in (2.5cm)

Finished Size:
1.75 in (4cm) wide x 3 in (7cm) tall

Stitch Guide:
See glossary for chain and single crochet.

Instructions:

Earring (make 2):

Row 1: With both yarns held together, ch10, sc in 2nd ch from hook, ch7, sc in last ch.

Row 2: Ch1, sc in same st, ch7, sc in last st.

Rows 3 - 10: Rep row 2. Fasten off.

Assembly:
Using pliers, open jump ring by twisting side to side. Insert french hook and beg ch10. Close jump ring by twisting. Repeat for second earring.

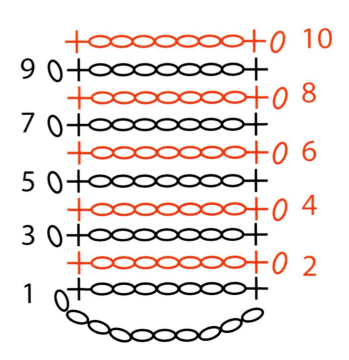

OLIVIA
Shawl

This is a simple, top down increase crochet shawl that is elevated with a swagged edging and beads. The pattern is easy to memorize after a few rows. It is beautiful in one color or in stripes of several of your favorite colors.

What you will need:

- 650 yds (594m) #1 superfine, fingering weight yarn
- G/6 (4mm) crochet hook
- 8 love knot beads, 10mm
- Yarn needle
- Scissors

Shown in:
Be So Fine Yarn; 100% bamboo; 650 yds (594m) per 4oz (113g); colors Passionate Plum, Stormy Sea, Chantilly Lace, Sun Kissed Yellow, Lilac Memories (130 yds or 119m used per color)

Gauge:
6 repeats of pattern = 4 in (10cm) wide x 3 in (7cm) tall after blocking

Finished Size:
54 in (137cm) wide x 27 in (69cm) tall

Special Stitch Instructions:
See Glossary for bead chain, chain, and double crochet.

Instructions:

Row 1: Ch5, (dc, ch2)x4 in 5th ch from hook, dc in same ch. -- 5 ch2 sps

Row 2: Ch5 (counts as dc, ch2), (dc, ch2, dc) in first ch2 sp, (dc, ch2, dc) in next ch2 sp, (dc, ch2, dc, ch2, dc, ch2, dc) in next ch2 sp, (dc, ch2, dc) in next ch2 sp, (dc, ch2, dc, ch2, dc) in last ch2 sp. -- 9 ch2 sps

Note: Each row from 3 to 32 is a repeat of row 2, except you are increasing by 4 ch2 sps (2 ch2 sps on ea side of center).

Row 3: Ch5 (counts as dc, ch2), (dc, ch2, dc) in first ch2 sp, (dc, ch2, dc) in ea of next 3 ch2 sps, (dc, ch2, dc, ch2, dc, ch2, dc) in next ch2 sp, (dc, ch2, dc) in ea of next 3 ch2 sps, (dc, ch2, dc, ch2, dc) in last ch2 sp. -- 13 ch2 sps

Rows 4 - 32: Rep row 2,

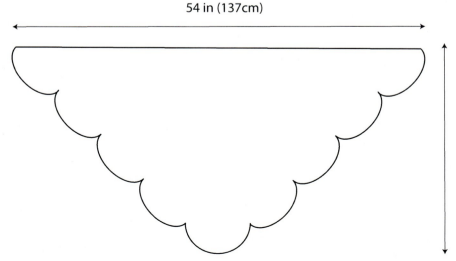

continuing in established pattern. -- 132 ch2 sps

Edging:

Row 33: Ch1, 4sc in first ch2 sps, *(4sc in next ch2 sp)x12, 1sc in next ch2 sp 6 rows below, bead chain*. Rep from * to * 4 more times. (4sc in next ch2 sp) x25, 1sc in next ch2 sp 6 rows below. Bead chain. Rep from * to * 4 more times. (4sc in next ch2 sp) x12. Fasten off.

Finishing:

Weave in loose ends. Hand wash, block to finished measurements and allow to dry.

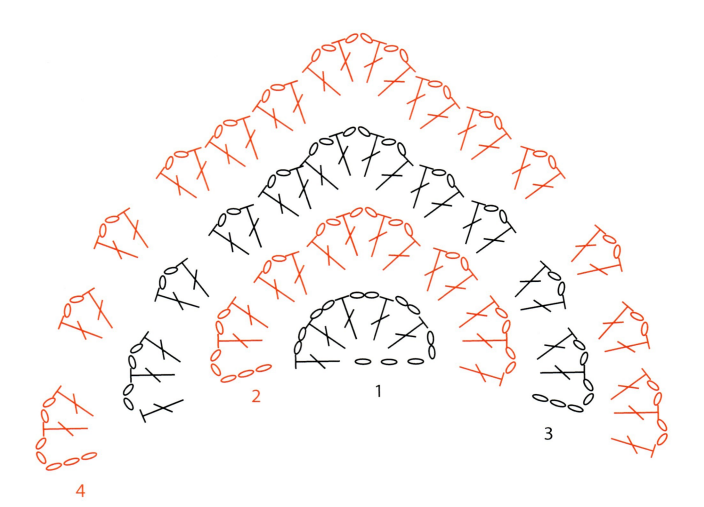

FELICIA

Mobius Cowl

This stitch pattern's loft and texture add sophistication to a simple mobius cowl. Choose a signature color to frame the face of your loved one.

What you will need:

- 325 yds (297m) #2 sport weight yarn
- H/8 (5mm) crochet hook
- Yarn needle
- Scissors

Shown in:
Be So Sporty Yarn; 100% bamboo; 325 yds (297m) per 4oz (113g); color Passionate Plum

Gauge:
18 sts / 8 rows = 4 in (10cm) in pattern after blocking

Finished Size:
25 in (63cm) circumference x 10 in (25cm) tall

Special Stitch Instructions:

See Glossary for chain, half double crochet and half double crochet through back loop.

Instructions:

Row 1: Ch47, hdc in 3rd ch from hook and ea ch across. -- 45 hdc

Row 2: Ch2 (does not count as st), hdc-tbl in ea st across. -- 45 hdc-tbl

Rows 3 - 50: Rep row 2. Fasten off, leaving long tail for seaming mobius.

Assembly: fold in half, twisting one time before seaming, so that you are joining the end of the last row with the beginning of the first row, joining corner A to corner D and corner B to corner C per the schematic.

Finishing:

Weave in loose ends. Hand wash, block to finished measurements and allow to dry.

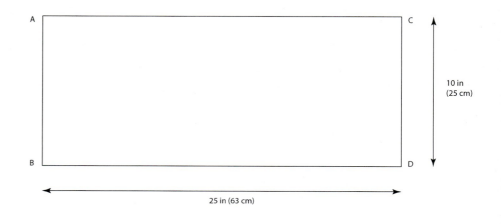

LEXI
Washcloth

Washcloths are a great extension of swatching for new stitches, and the efforts result in a great gifting opportunity. Combine a set of washcloths with organic soaps and bath bombs for a thoughtful spa gift.

What you will need:

- 315 yds (288m) #2 sport weight yarn
- G/6 (4mm) crochet hook
- Yarn needle
- Scissors

Shown in:
Be So Bare Yarn; 100% organic cotton; 315 yds (288m) per 4oz (113g); color undyed

Gauge:
24 sts / 12 rows = 4 in (10cm) in double crochet

Finished Size:
10 in (25cm) square

Stitch Guide:
See glossary for chain, single crochet, double crochet and slip stitch.

Instructions:

Increasing section:

Row 1: Ch6, 1dc in 4th ch from hook and ea ch across. -- 3 dcs

Row 2: Ch6, 1dc in 4th ch from hook and ea of next 2 chs, work (slst, ch3, 3dc) in ch3 sp on prev row. -- 6 dcs

Row 3: Ch6, (1dc in 4th ch from hook and ea of next 2 chs, *work (slst, ch3, 3dc) in next ch3 sp on prev row. Rep from * once more. -- 9 dcs

Row 4: Ch6, 1dc in 4th ch from hook and ea of next 2 chs, *work (slst, ch3, 3dc) in next ch3 sp on prev row. Rep from * two more times. -- 12 dcs

Row 5: Ch6, 1dc in 4th ch from hook and ea of next 2 chs, *work (slst, ch3, 3dc) in next ch3 sp on prev row. Rep from * three more times. -- 15 dcs

Rows 6 - 15: rep row 5, working in established pattern of increasing by 3 dcs ea row. -- 45 dcs

Decreasing section:

Row 16: Slst across ea of next 3 dcs, ch3, work 3dc in side of ch3 sp on prev row. *Work (slst ch3, 3dc) in next ch3 sp on prev row. Rep from * twelve more times. -- 42 dcs

Row 17: Slst across ea of next 3 dcs, ch3, work 3dc in side of ch3 sp on prev row. *Work (slst ch3, 3dc) in next ch3 sp on prev row. Rep from * eleven more times. -- 39 dcs

Rows 18 - 29: Rep row 17, working in established pattern of decreasing by 3 dcs ea row. -- 3 dcs

Edging:

Row 1: Ch3 (counts as dc), 1dc in ea of next 2 sts, *3dc in next ch3 sp, 1dc in ea of next 3 sts. Rep from * six more times, ch3. Rep from * three more times, slst to top of first st at beg of round to join. Fasten off.

Finishing:

Weave in loose ends. Hand wash, block to finished measurements and allow to dry.

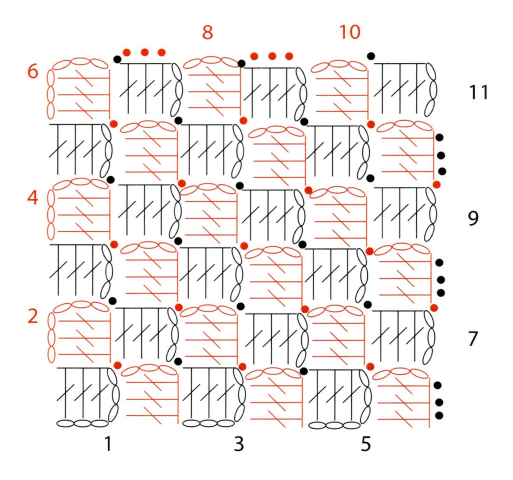

KATE

Trivet

Trivets are a universal gift that anyone with a kitchen can use. Think about the accent colors in someone's kitchen when choosing yarn colors. My kitchen has turquoise accents and orange is a great complement to turquoise.

What you will need:

- 120 yds (109m) #4 worsted weight yarn
- H/8 (5mm) crochet hook
- Yarn needle
- Scissors

Shown in:
Be So Brave Yarn; 100% American merino wool; 120 yds (109m) per 2oz (56g); color Orangesicle

Gauge:
Gauge is not critical for this project.

Finished Size:
13 in (33cm) diameter before felting

11 in (28cm) diameter after felting

Stitch Guide:

See Glossary for chain, single crochet, double crochet, and 3tr-cluster.

Instructions:

Round 1: Ch5, slst to 5th ch to form ring, Ch3 (counts as dc) work 15dc in ring, slst to top of first st at beg of round to join. -- 16 sts

Round 2: Ch4 (counts as dc, ch1), *dc, ch1, rep from * around. -- 16 sts, 16 ch1 sps

Round 3: Slst into next ch1 sp, ch4 (counts as dc, ch1), dc in same sp, (dc, ch1, dc) in ea ch1 sp around. Slst to top of first st at beg of round to join. -- 32 sts, 16 ch1 sps

Round 4: slst into next ch1 sp, ch3 (counts as dc), work (dc, ch2, 2dc) in same sp, work (2dc, ch2, 2dc) in ea ch1 sp around. Slst to top of first st at beg of round to join. -- 16 shells

Rounds 5 - 6: Rep round 4, except each shell is worked into the ch2 sp on the prev round.

Round 7: Slst into next ch1 sp, ch3 (counts as dc), work (2dc, ch2, 3dc) in same sp, work (3dc, ch2, 3dc) in ea ch2 sp around. Slst to top of first st at beg of round to join. -- 16 shells

Round 8: Slst into next ch1 sp, ch3 (counts as dc), work (3dc, ch2, 4dc) in same sp, work (4dc, ch2, 4dc) in ea ch2 sp around. Slst to top of first st at beg of round to join. -- 16 shells

Round 9: Rep round 8.

Round 10: Sc in same join, *ch4, 3tr-cluster in same sp, in next ch2 sp work (sc, ch2, 3dc, ch2, sc), ch4, 3tr-cluster in same sp, sc in sp between 2 shells. Rep from * around. Slst to top of first st at beg of round to join. Fasten off.

Finishing:

Weave in loose ends. Place in a lingerie bag. Wash with a small amount of soap in a hot/cold wash, along with some towels or other items to provide friction. Block and allow to dry.

SAMI
Trivet

A trivet can be used in a kitchen or on a dining room table, or even to liven things up when setting out platters on a coffee table. Embrace bright colors - they bring the sunshine inside!

What you will need:

- 200 yds (183m) #4 worsted weight yarn
- H/8 (5mm) crochet hook
- Yarn needle
- Scissors

Shown in:
Be So Brave Yarn; 100% American merino wool; 120 yds (109m) per 2oz (56g); color Orangesicle

Gauge:
24 sts / 12 rows = 4 in (10cm) in double crochet

Finished Size:
13 in (33cm) square, before felting

11 in (28cm) diameter after felting

Stitch Guide:

See glossary for beg 3tr-cluster, chain, single crochet, double crochet and slip stitch.

Instructions:

Ch5, slst to 5th ch from hook to form ring.

Round 1: Ch6 (counts as dc, ch3), (dc, ch3)x3 in ring, slst to top of first st at beg of round to join. -- 4 dcs, 4 ch3 sps

Round 2: Ch3 (counts as dc), (2dc, ch1, 3dc) in ch3 sp, *ch1, 3dc in next ch3 sp. Rep from * five more times. -- 8 ch1 sps, 24 sts

Round 3: Ch6 (counts as dc, ch3), work (dc, ch3, dc) in next ch1 sp, *ch3, dc in next ch1 sp, (ch3, dc)x2 in next ch1 sp. Rep from * around, replace last dc with slst to top of first st at beg of round to join. -- 12 ch3 sps, 12 dcs

Round 4: Slst into first ch3 sp, ch3 (counts as dc), 2dc in same sp, ch1, (3dc, ch1, 3dc) in next ch3 sp, *(ch1, 3dc in next ch3 sp)x2, (ch1, 3dc)x2 in next ch3 sp. Rep from * around, ch1, 3dc in next ch3 sp, ch1, slst to top of first st at beg of round to join. -- 48 dcs, 20 ch1 sps

Round 5: Ch6 (counts as dc, ch3), dc in next ch1 sp, (ch3, dc)x2 in next ch1 sp, *(ch3, dc in next ch1 sp)x3, (ch3, dc)x2 in next ch 1sp. Rep from *around, (ch3, dc in next ch1 sp, ch3, slst to top of first st at beg of round

to join. -- 20 dcs, 20 ch3 sps

Round 6: Slst into first ch3 sp, ch3 (counts as dc), 2dc in same sp, ch1, (3dc, ch1, 3dc) in next ch3 sp, *ch1, 3dc in next ch3 sp)x4, (ch1, 3dc)x2 in next ch3 sp. Rep from * around, ch1, 3dc in next ch3 sp, ch1, slst to top of first st at beg of round to join. -- 72 dcs, 24 ch1 sps

Rounds 7 - 12: Rep rounds 5 - 6 three more times.

Edging round: Ch1, sc in ch1 sp, *(beg 3tr-cluster, sc in next ch1 sp)x5, (ch2, dc, ch2, sc) in same ch1 sp, (beg 3tr cluster, sc in next ch1 sp)x7. Rep from * around, slst to top of first st at beg of round to join. -- 48 clusters, 4 corners

Finishing:

Weave in loose ends. Place in a lingerie bag. Wash with a small amount of soap in a hot/cold wash, along with some towels or other items to provide friction. Block and allow to dry

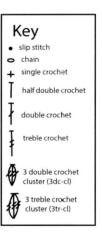

NICOLE
Washcloth

A round washcloth is a lovely variation on a traditional theme. Line a basket with a pretty set, and include some soaps and bath salts for a special gift. Or make some to pamper yourself!

What you will need:

- 300 yds (274m) #2 fine, sport weight yarn
- G/6 (4mm) crochet hook
- Stitch Marker
- Yarn needle
- Scissors

Shown in:
1 ball **Be So Bare Yarn**; 100% organic cotton; 315 yds (288m) per 4oz (113g); color undyed

Gauge:
24 sts / 12 rows = 4 in (10cm) in double crochet

Finished Size:
10 in (25cm) diameter

Stitch Guide:

See glossary for Beg 3tr-cluster, chain, single crochet, double crochet and slip stitch.

Instructions:

Ch5, slst to 5th ch from hook to form ring.

Round 1: Ch4 (counts as dc, ch1), (dc, ch1)x7 in ring, ch1, slst to top of first st at beg of round to join. -- 8 dcs, 8 ch1 sps

Round 2: Ch3 (counts as dc), 2dc in same st, (ch1, 3dc in next dc)x7, ch1, slst to top of first st at beg of round to join. -- 8 3dc sections, 8 ch1 sps

Round 3: Ch1, sc in same st, *ch7, skip 1 st, sc in next st, sc in next ch1 sp, sc in next st. Rep from * around, slst to top of first st at beg of round to join. -- 8 ch7 sps, 8 3sc sections

Round 4: Ch1, *in ch7 sp work (sc, hdc, 2dc, 5tr, 2dc, hdc, sc). Rep from * around, slst to top of first st at beg of round to join. -- 8 shells

Round 5: Slst in ea of next 5 sts, ch3 (counts as dc), dc in same st, (2dc, ch3, 2dc) in next st, 2dc in next st, *ch3, 2dc in next st, (2dc, ch3, 2dc) in next st, 2dc in next st. Rep from * around, ch1, hdc in first st at beg of round to join. Last (ch1, hdc) counts as last ch3 sp. -- 8 shells, 8 ch3 sps

Round 6: Ch7 (counts as tr, ch3), *(dc, ch3 dc) in next ch3 sp, ch3, (tr, ch3, tr) in next ch3 sp, ch3. Rep from * around, ch3, (dc, ch3, dc) in next ch3 sp, ch3, tr in last ch3 sp, ch1, hdc in 4th of beg ch to join. -- 32 ch3 sps

Edging:

Row 1: Ch8, hdc in 3rd ch from hook and ea ch across, slst in last ch3 sp on prev round, turn. -- 7 sts

Row 2: Hdc-tbl in ea st across. -- 7 sts

Row 3: Ch2 (counts as hdc), hdc-tbl in ea st across, slst in same ch3 sp as round 1. -- 7 sts

Row 4: Rep row 2

Row 5: Ch2 (counts as hdc), hdc-tbl in ea st across, slst in next ch3 sp on round 6. -- 7 sts

Row 6: Rep row 2

Row 7: Ch2 (counts as hdc), hdc-tbl in ea st across, slst in next ch3 sp on round 6. -- 7 sts

Row 8: Rep row 2.

Row 9: Ch2 (counts as hdc), hdc-tbl in ea st across, slst in same ch3 sp as row 7. -- 7 sts

Rep rows 4 - 9 until you have joined the edging to each ch3 sp around. Slst to join each st on last row to adjacent beg ch from row 1.

Finishing:

Weave in loose ends. Hand wash, block to finished measurements and allow to dry.

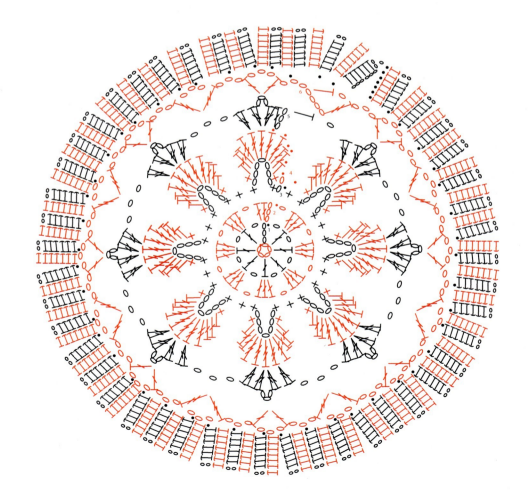

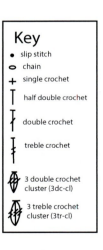

MIMI
Lace Candle Holder

Lace candle holders are an easy-to-make and universally appealing gift. The flameless votive makes it safe for all ages.

What you will need:
- 4, 5½, or 8 in (10, 14, 20cm) glass bubble vase
- Flameless votive candle
- 75 (100, 150) yds or (69, 91, 137m) #1 fingering weight yarn
- Size E/4 (3.5mm) crochet hook, or size to obtain correct gauge
- Yarn needle

Shown in:
Be So Fine Yarn; 100% bamboo; 650 yds (594m) per 4oz (113g); color Iced Silver Fox

Gauge:
1 rep of lace pattern is 1.5 in (4cm) wide

Finished Size:
Fits 4, 5½, 8 in (10, 14, 20cm) glass bubble vase

Stitch Guide:
See Glossary for dc3tog, chain, single crochet, double crochet, half double crochet, and slst.

Instructions:

Note: The last round of each Candle Holder pattern is worked with piece fitted onto vase.

Ch 5, sl st in first ch to make a ring.

Symbol Key
- ○ ch
- + sc
- T hdc
- ϯ dc
- ⩘ dc3tog
- • sl st
- ○ marker

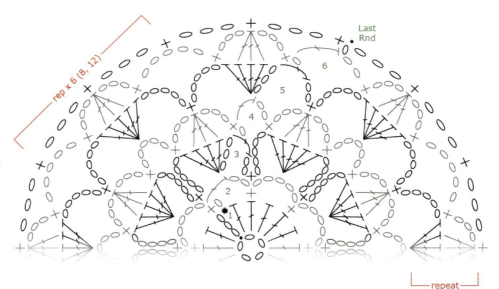

Round 1: Ch3 (counts as 1 dc), work 11 (15, 23) more dc in ring, join with slst in top of beg ch3. -- 12 (16, 24) dc.

Round 2: Ch1, sc in same st as joining slst, * ch5, sk next st, sc in next st; rep from * 4 (6, 10) more times, ch2, join with dc in first sc (last ch2, dc count as last ch5 sp here and throughout). -- 6 (8, 12) ch-5 sps

Round 3: Ch3 (counts as 1 dc), 4 dc in same st as joining dc, * ch5, sc in next sc, ch5, 5 dc in center ch of next ch5 sp; rep from * 4 (6, 10) more times, ch5, sc in next sc, ch2, join with dc in top of beg ch3. -- 12 (16, 24) ch-5 sps.

Round 4: Ch1, sc in sp formed by join, * ch3, sk next dc, dc3tog over next 3 dc, ch3, sc in next ch5 sp, ch5, sc in next ch5 sp; rep from * 4 (6, 10) more times, ch3, sk next dc, dc3tog over next 3 dc, ch3, sc in next ch5 sp, ch2, join with dc in first sc. -- 6 (8, 12) dc3tog

Round 5: Ch3 (counts as 1 dc), 4 dc in same st as joining dc, * ch5, sc in next dc3tog, ch5, 5 dc in center ch of next ch5 sp; rep from * 4 (6, 10) more times, ch5, sc in next dc3tog, ch2, join with dc in top of beg ch3. -- 12 (16, 24) ch5 sps

Round 6: Rep round 4.

Rep rounds 5 and 6 until it fits the vase with a little stretch, ending after a round 6.

Note: Last round is worked while crochet is stretched onto the glass vase to create a decreased lip to hold it securely in place.

Last round: Ch 1, sc in sp formed by join, * ch3, sc in next dc3tog, ch3, sc in next ch5 sp; rep from * 4 (6, 10) more times, ch3, sc in next dc3tog, ch 3, join with slst in first sc. -- 12 (16, 24) ch3 sps

Fasten off.

Finishing:

Weave in loose ends. Place flameless votive candle inside.

MELANIE
Lace Candle Holder

Make a gift set in the various patterns for a glamorous gift. Or incorporate them into the centerpieces of a big party or wedding reception.

What you will need:

- 4, 5½, or 8 in (10, 14, 20cm) glass bubble vase
- Flameless votive candles
- 75 (100, 150) yds or (69, 91, 137m) #1 fingering weight yarn
- Size E/4 (3.5mm) crochet hook, or size to obtain correct gauge
- Yarn needle
- Stitch markers

Shown in:
Be So Fine Yarn; 100% bamboo; 650 yds (594m) per 4oz (113g); color Chantilly Lace

Gauge:
1 rep of lace pattern is 1.5 in (4cm) wide

Finished Size:
Fits 4 (5½, 8)" glass bubble vase

Stitch Guide:
See Glossary for single crochet, chain and slip stitch.

Instructions:

Ch 5, sl st in first ch to make a ring.

Round 1: * Ch3, sc in ring, ch5, sc in ring; rep from * twice more, ch3, sc in ring, ch2, dc in ring (last ch2 and dc count as last ch5 sp here and throughout) – 4 ch5 sps.

Round 2: Ch3, sc in sp formed by join, * ch5, (sc, ch3, sc, ch5, sc, ch3, sc) all in next ch5 sp; rep from * twice more, ch5, (sc, ch3, sc, ch2, dc) in first sp of round to join – 8 ch5 sps.

Mark sp formed by join, and in every other ch5 sp – 4 markers.

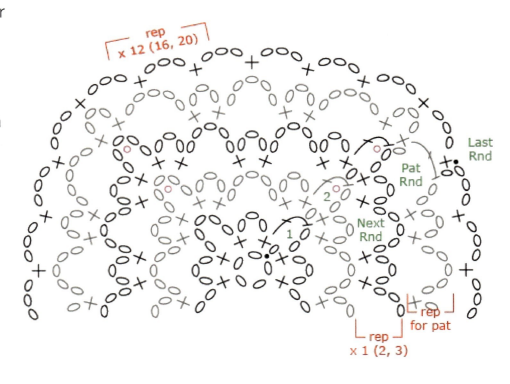

Next 1 (2, 3) rounds: Ch 1, (sc, ch3, sc) in sp formed by join, * (ch5, sc, ch3, sc) in each ch5 sp to marked ch5 sp, ch5, (sc, ch3, sc, ch5, sc, ch3, sc) in marked sp; rep from * twice more, (ch5, sc, ch3, sc) in each ch5 sp to first sp of round (marked), ch5, (sc, ch3, sc, ch2, dc) in first sp of round to join – 12 (16, 20) ch5 sps. Move each marker to sp directly above it.

Next round: Ch 1, (sc, ch3, sc) in sp formed by join, * ch5, (sc, ch3, sc) in next ch5 sp; rep from * around, ch2, dc in first sp of round to join – 12 (16, 20) ch5 sps.

Rep last round until it fits the vase with a little stretch.

Note: The last round is worked while crochet is stretched onto the glass vase to create a decreased lip to hold it securely in place.

Last round: Ch 1, sc in sp formed by join, * ch3, sc in next ch5 sp; rep from * around, join with sl st in first sc. Fasten off.

Finishing:

Weave in loose ends. Place flameless votive candle inside.

CAROLINE
Lace Candle Holder

Make a set in the various sizes for a fabulous housewarming gift. This is one of my favorite gifts to make for a new home celebration.

What you will need:

- 4, 5½, or 8 (10, 14, 20cm) glass bubble vase
- Flameless votive candles
- 75 (100, 150) yds or (69, 91, 137m) #1 fingering weight yarn
- Size E/4 (3.5mm) crochet hook, or size to obtain correct gauge
- Yarn needle

Shown in:
Be So Fine Yarn; 100% bamboo; 650 yds (594m) per 4oz (113g); color Million Dollar Red

Gauge:
1 rep of lace pattern is 1.5 in (4cm) wide

Finished Size:
Fits 4, 5½, 8 in (10, 14, 20cm) glass bubble vase

Stitch Guide:
See glossary for chain, single crochet, slip stitch, half double crochet, and double crochet.

Instructions:

Ch 5, sl st in first ch to make a ring.

Round 1: Ch3 (counts as 1 dc), work 11 (15, 23) more dc in ring, join with sl st in top of beg ch3 – 12 (16, 24) dc.

Round 2: Ch1, sc in same st as joining sl st, * ch5, sk next st, sc in next st; rep from * 4, 6, 10 more times, ch2, join with dc in first sc (last ch2, dc count as last ch5 sp) – 6 (8, 12) ch5 sps.

Round 3: Ch3 (counts as 1 dc), 3 dc in sp formed by join, * (4 dc, ch2, 4 dc) in next ch5 sp; rep from * 4 (6, 10) more times, 4 dc in

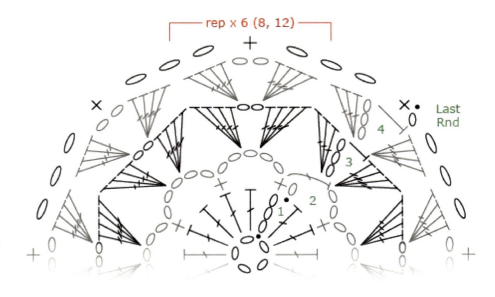

first sp of round, join with hdc in top of beg ch3 (hdc counts as last ch2 sp here and throughout) – 6 (8, 12) shells.

Round 4: Ch3 (counts as 1 dc), 3 dc in sp formed by join, * (4 dc, ch2, 4 dc) in next ch2 sp; rep from * 4 (6, 10) more times, 4 dc in first sp of round, join with hdc in top of beg ch3 (hdc counts as last ch2 sp here and throughout) – 6 (8, 12) shells.

Last round: Ch 1, sc in sp formed by join, * ch3, sc in next ch2 sp; rep from * around, join with sl st in first sc.
Fasten off.

Note: The last round of each Candle Holder pattern is worked with piece fitted onto vase.

Finishing:

Weave in loose ends. Place flameless votive candle inside.

GABI
Lace Candle Holder

Lace candle holders are an easy-to-make and universally appealing gift. When making a set, choose thematic or complementary colors. For a more festive look, add some metallic beads.

What you will need:

- 4, 5½, or 8 in (10, 14, 20cm) glass bubble vase
- Flameless votive candles
- 75 (100, 150) yds or (69, 91, 137m) #1 fingering weight yarn
- Size E/4 (3.5mm) crochet hook, or size to obtain correct gauge
- Yarn needle

Shown in:
Be So Fine Yarn; 100% bamboo; 650 yds (594m) per 4oz (113g); color Pure Gold

Gauge:
1 rep of lace pattern is 1.5 in (4cm) wide

Finished Size:
Fits 4 (5½, 8) in (10, 14, 20cm) glass bubble vase

Stitch Guide:
See Glossary for chain, single crochet, half double crochet, double crochet, dc3tog, and slst.

Instructions:

Note: The last round of each Candle Holder pattern is worked with piece fitted onto vase.

Ch5, sl st in first ch to make a ring.

Round 1: Ch3 (counts as 1 dc), work 11 (19, 23) more dc in ring, join with sl st in top of beg ch3. – 12 (20, 24) dc.

Round 2: Ch1, sc in same st as joining sl st, * ch5, sk next st, sc in next st; rep from * 4 (8, 10) more times, ch5, join with sl st in first sc. – 6 (10, 12) ch-5 sps.

Round 3: Ch1, sc in same

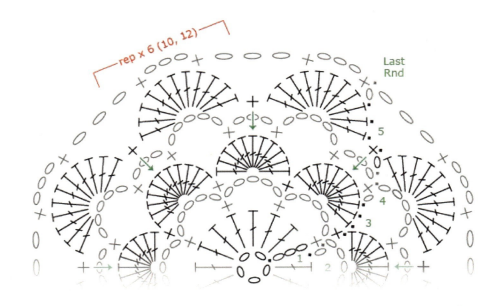

st as joining sl st, *11 dc in next ch5 sp, sc in next sc; rep from * 4 (8, 10) more times, 11 dc in next ch5 sp, join with sl st in first sc. – 6 (10, 12) scales.

Round 4: Slst in each of next 3 dc, ch1, *sc in next dc, ch3, sk 3 dc, sc in next dc, ch5, sk 7 sts; rep from * 5 (9, 11) more times, join with sl st in first sc. – 6 (10, 12) ch-3 sps.

Round 5: Slst in next ch3 sp, ch1, * working in front of ch3, sc in center dc of 3 skipped dc of 2 rounds ago, 11 dc in next ch5 sp; rep from * 5 (9, 11) more times – 6 (10, 12) scales.

Rep rounds 4 and 5 until it fits the vase with a little stretch, ending after a rnd 5.

Last round: Slst in each of next 3 dc, * sc in next dc, ch3, sk 3 dc, sc in next dc, ch3, sk 7 sts; rep from * 5 (9, 11) more times, join with sl st in first sc. – 12 (20, 24) ch-3 sps.

Finishing:

Weave in loose ends. Place flameless votive candle inside.

GRACE

Crochet Bracelet

This bracelet has a braided texture that is deceptively simple to make with slip stitches. The gorgeous, Czech glass button and sparkly yarn add elegance and glamour.

What you will need:

- 150 yds (137m) #2 sport weight yarn
- E/4 (3.5mm) crochet hook Yarn needle
- Scissors
- Sewing needle
- Thread
- 25mm Czech glass button

Shown in:
Be So Sporty BLING Yarn; 90 % bamboo, 10% silver; 300 yds (274m) per 4oz (113g); color Mermaid 01

Gauge:
20 sts / 32 rows = 4 in (10cm) in slst braid stitch pattern

Finished Size:
7 in (18cm) long

Stitch Guide

See Glossary for chain, slst and slst-tbl.

Instructions:

Ch 70, slst to join in a ring being careful not to twist chain.

Round 1: Slst-tbl in ea ch around. -- 70 sts

Round 2: Slst-tbl in ea st around. -- 70 sts

Rounds 3 - 5: Rep round 2.

Fasten off.

Finishing:

Weave in loose ends. Sew button to one end of loop, with right side facing. Bracelet is worn with loop folded in half and one side wrapped over the button to secure.

7 in (18cm)

RACHEL

Crochet Necklace

This necklace has a braided texture that is deceptively simple to make with slip stitches. You can add a ring or pendant with a slip knot or with a jump ring as shown.

What you will need:

- 200 yds (183m) #2 sport weight yarn
- E/4 (3.5mm) crochet hook Yarn needle
- Scissors
- 12cm jump ring
- 2 pairs of chain nose pliers
- 25mm glass pendant

Shown in:
Be So Sporty BLING Yarn; 90 % bamboo, 10% silver; 300 yds (274m) per 4oz (113g); color Mermaid 01

Gauge:

20 sts / 32 rows = 4 in (10cm) in slst braid stitch pattern

Finished Size:

28 in (71cm) circumference

Stitch Guide

See Glossary for chain, slst and slst-tbl.

Instructions:

Ch 140, slst to join in a ring being careful not to twist chain.

Round 1: Slst-tbl in ea ch around. -- 140 sts

Round 2: Slst-tbl in ea st around. -- 140 sts

Rounds 3 4: Rep round 2. Fasten off.

Finishing:

Weave in loose ends. Open jump ring, place pendant on ring, and wrap ring around entire loop of necklace being careful to position the pendant to be right side facing with the necklace. Close ring.

AMANDA

Crochet Lariat Necklace

A lariat-style necklace is incredibly easy to make and wear. The pizazz is all in the materials! The weight of the beads at the ends of the chains gives the necklace great body. Whether you match your yarn and pendant or choose contrasting colors, your options are unlimited!

What you will need:

- 100 yds (92m) #2 sport weight yarn
- G/6 (4mm) crochet hook
- Yarn needle
- Scissors
- (1) 55mm x 35mm acrylic pendant, speckled purple
- (6) 8mm x 6mm ornate large hole metal tube charm beads

Shown in:
Be So Fine Yarn; 100% bamboo; 650 yds (597m) per 4oz (113g); color Lilac Memories

Be So Dazzling Yarn; 100% polyester; 100yds per 25g spool, color silver

Gauge:

16 ch = 4 in (10cm)

Finished Size:

Each chain is 60 in (152cm) long

Stitch Guide

See glossary for chain.

Instructions:

Chains (make 3)

With both yarns held together, ch140. Fasten off.

Finishing:

Weave in loose ends. Thread a metal charm bead onto end of each chain. Tie a double knot in end of each chain to secure bead. Holding all chains together, fold in half and thread fold through hole in pendant. Secure pendant with a slip knot. Slide each chain through the hole in pendant to make a sliding lariat.

LIZ
Crochet Necklace

This very fine gauge crochet chain has the delicate look of metal chains. The gorgeous lampwork pendant is the focal point. A completely different look can be achieved by crocheting small crystal beads into the chain.

What you will need:

- 215 yds (196m) #1 fingering weight yarn
- B/1 (2.25mm) crochet hook
  Yarn needle
- Scissors
- (1) 2.5 in (63mm) lampwork glass mermaid tail pendant

Shown in:
Be So Fine Yarn; 100% bamboo; 650 yds (594m) per 4oz (113g); color Pure Gold

Instructions:

Chain:
Chain 24 in (94cm) for every strand of necklace you desire. The sample is 8 strands, for a total of 192 in (487cm) or 16 ft (5.3 yds or 4.9 m). Fasten off, leaving a 24 in (94cm) tail for assembly.

Assembly:
Using 24 in (94cm) as your guide and working on a flat surface, insert one tail of long chain through the pendant, and make a 24 in (94cm) loop on the table. Working with opposite end of chain, *insert tail through pendant, slide all the way through, and make an identical loop over the first 24 in (94cm) loop on the table. Rep from * until you have all 8 loops threaded through the pendant and 8 similar 24 in (94cm) loops on the table. Undo the fastened off side of the chain and put the last chain back on crochet hook. Slst into first ch at opposite end. Slst in ea of the next 4 sts. Holding all 8 chains together, sc around all together. Work 18 more sc. Fasten off.

Finishing:
Weave in loose ends.

Gauge:
Gauge is not critical for this project but 32 chs = 4 in (10cm)

Finished Size:
24 in (94cm) circumference

Stitch Guide
See Glossary for chain and single crochet.

KELLY

Earrings

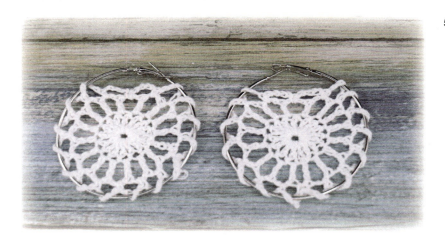

Taking a simple crochet motif and framing it in hoop earrings is an easy project to make. These earrings are dramatic, on trend and gorgeous. Make them in any color!

What you will need:

- 50 yds (45m) #1 superfine, fingering weight yarn
- C/2 (2.75mm) crochet hook
- (2) 2.25 in (6cm) hoop earrings
- Yarn needle
- Scissors
- E6000 craft adhesive glue

Shown in:
Be So Fine Yarn; 100% bamboo; 650 yds (594m) per 4oz (113g); color Chantilly Lace

Gauge:
First round of motif = 1 in (2.5cm) diameter

Finished Size:
2.25 in (6cm) diameter after being stretched onto earring hoop

Stitch Guide:
See Glossary for chain, single crochet, double crochet, slip stitch.

Instructions:

Earring (make 2):

Ch5, slst to first ch to form ring.

Round 1: Ch3 (counts as dc), 15dc in ring. Slst to top of ch3 at beg of round to join. -- 16 dcs

Round 2: Ch4 (counts as dc, ch1), *dc in next st, ch1. Rep from * around, slst to top of ch3 at beg of round to join. -- 16 ch1 sps

Round 3: Ch1, sc in same st, *Ch3, sc in next dc. Rep from * around, except on last rep, replace sc with slst. Fasten off. Weave in loose ends.

Assembly:
Slide motif onto hoop earrings through the ch3 sps, leave the last 2 ch3 sps unjoined. Apply a dot of glue to each join to secure placement on earring. Allow to dry completely.

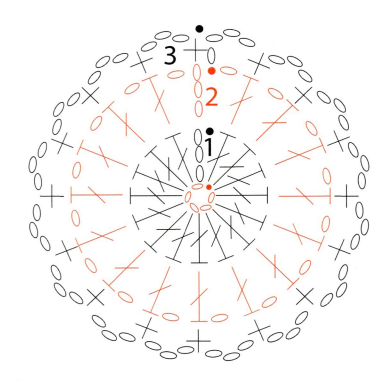

TANYA

Crochet Jar Topper

Making decorations for containers filled with gifts is such a lovely sentiment. The 3-dimensional flower is seamlessly joined to the jar topper.

What you will need:

- 140 yds (128m) #4 medium, worsted weight yarn
- H/8 (5mm) crochet hook
- Yarn needle
- Scissors
- 24 in (61cm) 1/2 in (13cm) wide ribbon

Shown in:
Be So Tender Yarn; 100% organic cotton; 140 yds (128m) per 3.5oz (100g); color Cloud

Gauge:
12 sts / 8 rows = 4 in (10cm) in double crochet

Finished Size:
To fit a standard Mason jar with 10 in (25cm) circumference

Stitch Guide

See Glossary for chain, single crochet, double crochet, treble crochet and slst.

Instructions:

Ch5, slst to 5th ch from ring to form ring.

Round 1: *Ch3, 4tr in ring, ch3, slst in ring. Rep from * 3 more times. -- 4 petals

Round 2: *Ch5, working behind petals of round 1, sc in next st. Rep from * 3 more times. -- 4 ch5 sps

Round 3: *(Slst, ch3, 6tr, ch3, slst) in next ch5 sp.

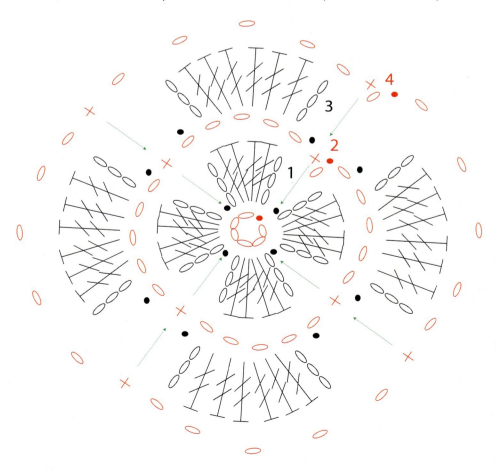

Rep from * 3 more times, slst to first slst at beg of round to join. -- 4 petals

Round 4: *Ch5, working behind petals of round 3, slst in sc on round 2. Rep from * around. -- 4 ch5 sps

Round 5: Slst into first ch5 sp, ch3 (counts as dc), 4dc in same ch5 sp. *5dc in next ch5 sp. Rep from * two more times, slst to first st at beg of round to join. -- 20 dcs

Round 6: Ch3 (counts as dc), dc in same st, 1dc in next st. *2dc in next st, 1dc in next st. Rep from * across. Slst to first st at beg of round to join. -- 30 dcs

Round 7: Ch3 (counts as dc), 1dc in next st, ch1, skip 1 st, *1dc in ea of next 2 sts, skip 1 st, ch1. Rep from * around, slst to top of ch3 at beg of round to join. -- 10 ch1 sps

Round 8: Ch3 (counts as dc), 1dc in ea st and ch around, slst to top of ch3 at beg of round to join. -- 30 dcs

Finishing:

Weave in loose ends. Weave ribbon through the eyelet holes on round 7.

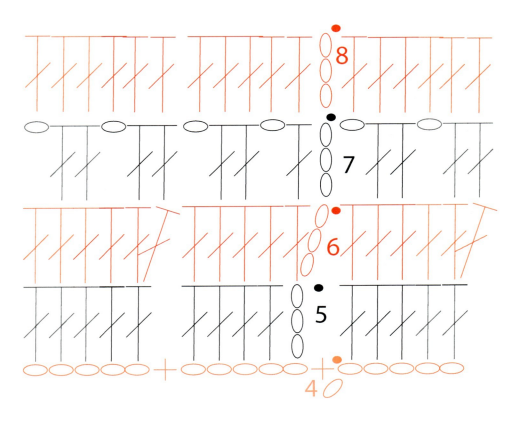

DANA
Heart Motif Earrings

A simple heart can be inserted into a card, a book, a lunch box, or a suitcase for an unexpected, any day surprise. If you prefer, use it to adorn a card or other project. And they can be easily transformed into festive earrings.

What you will need:

- 50 yds (45m) #1 fingering weight yarn
- Yarn needle
- Scissors
- B/1 (2.25mm) crochet hook
- (4) jump rings
- (2) french hooks
- (2) pairs of chain nose or bent nose pliers

Shown in:
Be So Fine Yarn; 100% bamboo; 650 yds (594m) per 4oz (113g); color Lavender's First Romance

Gauge:
Not critical for this project

Finished Size:
1.5 in (4cm) diameter motif

Stitch Guide

See Glossary for chain, single crochet, double crochet, treble crochet, double treble crochet and slip stitch.

Instructions:

Round 1: Ch6, slst to 6th ch from hook to form ring. Ch3 (counts as dc), (4dc, 1sc, 8dc, tr, dtr, tr, 4dc) in ring. Slst to top of ch3 at beg of round to join.

Row 2: Ch1, sc in same st, skip 1dc, 9dc in next st, skip 2 dcs, sc in next sc, skip 2 dcs, 9dc in next st. Do not turn. Do not complete round.

Round 3: Skip next dc, *ch1, slst in next st. Rep from * around.
Note: the third round begins at the opposite side of the heart as the end of round 1 because row 2 is only worked around half of round 1. Fasten off.

Finishing:

Weave in loose ends. Using pliers, open jump ring by twisting side to side. Insert french hook. Close jump ring by twisting. Open second jump ring and insert into top center of heart motif and first jump ring. Close jump ring by twisting. Repeat for second earring.

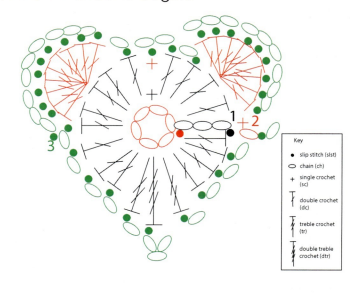

MAGGIE

Drawstring Bag

This elegant drawstring bag could be filled with goodies or even double as an evening purse. You could also add beads to the drawstrings.

What you will need:

- 325 yds (297m) #2 sport weight yarn
- US6 (4mm) circular knitting needles, 16 in (40cm) cord length
- US6 (4mm) double pointed needles for icord
- Stitch Marker
- Yarn needle
- Scissors

Shown in:
Be So Sporty BLING; 90% bamboo, 10% silver; 300 yds (274m) per 4oz (113g); color Sunrise 02

Gauge:
20 sts/ 24 rows = 4 in (10cm) in pattern

Finished Size:
9 in (23cm) wide x 10 in (25cm) tall

Stitch Guide:
See Glossary for knit, purl, CO, BO, kfb, kfbf, k2tog, k3tog.

Instructions:

Bag:

CO 96 sts, place stitch marker, join in a ring being careful not to twist. -- 96 sts

Round 1: *With yarn in front, slip 2 stitches to right hand needle, move yarn to back, slip same 2 stitches back to left hand needle, knit same 2 sts, k2. Repeat from * around. -- 96 sts

Round 2: Knit around. -- 96 sts

Round 3: *K2, with yarn in front, slip 2 sts to right hand needle, move yarn to back, slip same 2 sts back to left hand needle, knit same 2 sts. Rep from * around. -- 96 sts

Round 4: Knit around. -- 96 sts

Rounds 5 - 52: Rep rounds 1 - 4 twelve more times.

Drawstring holes:

Round 53: *K4, yo, k2tog. Rep from * around. -- 96 sts

Round 54: Knit around. -- 96 sts

Necklace top:

Rounds 55 - 56: *K2, p2. Rep from * around. -- 96 sts

Rounds 57 - 58: *P2, k2. Rep from * around. -- 96 sts

Rounds 59 - 66: Rep rounds 55 - 58 two more times.

Fasten off in pattern.

Icords (Make 2):

Round 1: Using double pointed needles, CO 1 sts, kfbf. -- 3 sts

Round 2: Slide sts to opposite end of knitting needle, k3. -- 3 sts

Rep round 2 until icord is 30 in (76cm) long.

Last round: K3tog. Fasten off.

Finishing:

Sew base of bag.

Thread one icord through the eyelet round (round 53), starting at eyelet directly above one corner of base seam. Thread the second icord throught the eyelet round of bag (round 53), starting at eyelet directly above the other corner of base seam. You should have ends of each icord coming out of opposite sides of bag. Tie each icord's tails together, 2 in (5cm) from end.

Weave in loose ends. Hand wash, block to finished measurements and allow to dry.

CALIOPE

Small Drawstring Bag

A mini bag can function as an organizer for a purse, suitcase or craft bag. Eyewear fits well. Or, it is a thoughtful way to wrap up another gift!

What you will need:

- 60 yds (55m) #4 worsted weight yarn
- 5 in (12.5cm) double pointed needles (set of 4) in size US 8 (5mm)
- Beads (optional)
- Stitch marker
- Yarn needle
- Scissors

Shown in:
Be So Brave Yarn; 100% American Merino Wool; 120 yds (109m) per 2oz (56g); color American Beauty

Gauge:
16 sts / 22 rows = 2 in (5cm) in stockinette stitch

Finished Size:
3 in (7.5cm) wide x 6 in (15cm) high

Stitch Guide:
See Glossary for cast on, knit, purl, yarn over, k2tog and 3 needle bind off.

Instructions:

CO 24 sts. Divide the stitches into thirds as follows: slip 8 sts onto ea of 2 needles purlwise, leaving 8 sts on the last needle. Slide the sts to the center of ea needle to prevent them from slipping off.

Note: Form a triangle with the 3 needles keeping the cast on ridge straight and not twisted around the needles.

Round 1: *K2, p2. Rep from * around, place marker. -- 24 sts

Rounds 2 - 6: Rep round 1.

Round 7: *K2, yo, k2tog. Rep from * around, slip marker. -- 24 sts

Rounds 8 - 9: *P2. k2, slip marker. -- 24 sts

Rounds 10 - 11: *K2, p2, slip marker. -- 24 sts

Rep rounds 8 - 11 until piece is 6 in (15cm) high.

Assembly:

Move the stitches evenly onto 2 needles as follows: slip the first 4 sts from the second needle onto the first needle and the remaining 4 sts onto the third needle. You should have 12 sts on ea of 2 needles. Holding needles parallel to each other, BO all sts with 3 needle bind off technique.

I-cord:

Round 1: CO 3 sts, *without turning the needle, slide the sts to the opposite end of the needle; holding the working yarn with a tight tension behind the work, k3. Rep from * until the cord measures approximately 12 in (30.5cm) from cast on edge. BO all sts leaving a long tail for sewing.

Using the long end of the cord, weave the cord through the eyelet row of the pouch; sew the ends of the cord together.

Finishing:

Hand wash, block to finished measurements and allow to dry.

CARRIE
Market Bag

Market bags are very useful and appeal to many different people. The elegant stitch pattern broadens the possibilities even more!

What you will need:

- 315 yds (288m) #2 sport weight yarn
- US6 (4mm) circular knitting needles, 16 in (40cm) cord length
- Yarn needle
- Scissors

Shown in:
Be So Serene Yarn; 100% organic cotton; 315 yds (288m) per 4oz (113g); color Zen

Gauge:
18 sts = 4 in (10cm) in blocked stitch pattern

Finished Size:
12 in (cm) wide x 10 in (25cm) tall, not including handles

Stitch Guide:
See Glossary for knit, purl, k2tog, CO, and BO.

Instructions:

Straps (make 2):

CO 54 sts. Knit 4 rows. BO all sts.

Bag:

Round 1: Pick up and knit 4 sts along narrow side edge of one strap, KCO 23 sts, pick up and knit 4 sts along opposite narrow side edge of strap, KCO 23 sts, pick up and knit 4 sts along narrow side edge of second strap, KCO 23 sts pick up and knit 4 sts along opposite narrow side edge of same strap, KCO 23 sts. Place marker, join in the round, being careful not to twist the sts. -- 108 sts

Round 2: Purl around. -- 108 sts

Round 3: Knit around. -- 108 sts

Round 4: Purl around. -- 108 sts

Round 5: *K2, yo, k1, yo, k2, ssk, k2tog. Rep from * around. -- 108 sts

Round 6 (and all even numbered rounds): Knit around. -- 108 sts

Round 7: *K2tog, k2, yo, k1, yo, k2, ssk. Rep from * around. -- 108 sts

Round 8: Remove st marker, k1, replace st marker, *k2, yo, k1, yo, k2, ssk, k2tog. Rep from * around. -- 108 sts

Rounds 9 - 52: Rep rounds 5 - 8 eleven more times.

Base:

Round 1: *K2tog, k1. Rep from * around. -- 72 sts

Rounds 2 - 4: Knit around. -- 72 sts

Round 5: K2tog around. -- 36 sts

Rounds 6 - 7: Knit around. -- 36 sts

Round 8: K2tog around. -- 18 sts.

Cut yarn, leaving long tail. Weave tail through all remaining sts, cinch, and fasten off.

Finishing:

Weave in loose ends. Hand wash, block to finished measurements and allow to dry.

COURTNEY
Bowl

If you can make a hat, you can make this visually stunning bowl. A completely hardened, textured knit makes this a unique home decor accessory.

What you will need:

- 140yds (130m) #4 worsted weight yarn
- US8 (5mm) knitting needles
- Yarn needle
- Scissors
- Smooth-On Smooth-Cast 325 Liquid Plastic
- Latex gloves
- Disposable bowl and stir stick
- Balloon or silicone mold (bowl shaped) with approximately 18 - 20 in (46 - 51cm) circumference

Shown in:
Be So Tender Yarn; 100% organic cotton; 140 yds (130m) per 3.5oz (100g); color Seafoam

Gauge:
12 sts / 16 rows = 4 in (10cm) in blocked basketweave stitch

Finished Size:
20 in (51cm) circumference x 9 in (23cm) tall

Stitch Guide:
See Glossary for knit, purl, k2tog and k3tog.

Instructions:

CO 60 sts

Row 1: *K3, p3. Rep from * across. -- 60 sts

Rows 2 - 4: Rep row 1

Row 5: *P3, k3. Rep from * across. -- 60 sts

Rows 6 - 8: Rep row 5

Rows 9 - 40: Rep rows 1 - 8 four more times.

Row 41: K3tog across. -- 20 sts

Row 42: Purl across. -- 20 sts

Row 43: K2tog across. -- 10 sts

Finishing:

Cut yarn leaving 18" long tail. Thread tail onto yarn needle and slide all 10 sts off knitting needle and through yarn needle. Cinch closed. Secure with a knot. Sew side edges bowl of together. Weave in loose ends.

Saturate in solution per manufacturer's instructions, squeeze out the excess solution, block to bowl shape and allow to dry.

CARLY
Lace Edged Napkin

A narrow strip of knit lace is easily attached to the edge of fabric with strategically placed picked up stitches at the end of each repeat. This is a fantastic opportunity for knitting on fabric to elevate a bandana into a fancy headscarf, a gift wrap for a homemade cake or a set of beautiful lace edged napkins.

What you will need:

- 70 yds (64m) #1 fingering weight yarn
- 1.0mm crochet hook
- US3 (3.25mm) knitting needles
- 22 in (56cm) cotton bandana
- Yarn needle
- Scissors

Shown in:
Be So Fine Yarn; 100% bamboo; 650 yds (594m) per 4oz (113g); color Chantilly Lace

Gauge:
ea repeat is 1.5 in (4cm) wide x 1 in (2.5cm) tall

Finished Size:
25 in (63cm) square bandana

Special Stitch Instructions:

See Glossary for knit, purl, k2tog, CO and BO.

Instructions:

Note: The smaller crochet hook is sharp enough to pierce this fabric directly for picking up stitches on the edge of the fabric to join to the last stitch of every other row of knitting.

CO 5 sts

Row 1: K2, yo twice, k2tog, k1. -- 6 sts

Row 2: K2, kfb, k2. -- 6 sts

Row 3: K4, yo twice, k2. -- 8 sts

Row 4: K2, kfb, k4. -- 8 sts

Row 5: K2, yo twice, k2tog,

Row 6: K5, kfb, k2. -- 9 sts

Row 7: K9. -- 9 sts

Row 8: BO 4 sts, k4, pick up a stitch along the edge of the fabric with the crochet hook and place it on the knitting needle. Pass the 2nd to last st up and over this last st. -- 5 sts

Rep rows 1 - 8 for perimeter of napkin, evenly placing the next join on ea row 8 approx 1 in (25cm) from last join. Join two repeats in each corner to add ease. BO all sts, leaving tail for sewing last row of sts to cast on edge.

Finishing:

Weave in loose ends. Hand wash, block to finished measurements and allow to dry.

CIARA
Skinny Scarf

A skinny scarf is a great introduction to learning a new and interesting stitch pattern. The openwork makes a beautiful scarf which can also be worn as a headscarf or sash belt.

What you will need:

- 247 yds (225m) #4 worsted weight yarn
- US8 (5mm) knitting needles
- Yarn needle
- Scissors

shown in:
Be So Bold Yarn; 51% organic cotton, 49% bamboo; 247 yds (225m) per 4oz (113g); color Mia's Malachite Meadow

Gauge:
20 sts / 12 rows = 4 in (10cm) in pattern after blocking

Finished Size:
3 in (7cm) wide x 68 in (173cm) long

Stitch Guide:
See Glossary for CO, knit, yarn over, and BO.

Instructions:

CO 17 sts

Row 1: K1, *k2, pass second st on right needle tip over first st, k1, pass second st on right needle tip over first st, sl1 purlwise with yarn in back, pass second st on right needle tip over first st (3 sts BO); rep from * across.-- 5 sts

Row 2: K1, *yo, k1. Rep from * across. 9 sts

Row 3: Knit across.

Row 4: K1, *k1 in the yo space below, k2. Rep from * aross. -- 13 sts

Row 5: K1, *k1 in the same yo space 2 rows below, k3. Rep from * across, ending last rep k2. -- 17 sts

Rows 6 - 225: Rep rows 1 - 5 forty-four more times. BO loosely.

Finishing:

Weave in loose ends. Hand wash, block to finished measurements and allow to dry.

ARIANNA

Earrings

The crescent-shaped motif and picot edging are deceptively simple to make. The picots are perfectly spaced for shaping the motif through the hoop earring and transforming the motifs into little stars.

What you will need:

- 25 yds (23)m #1 fingering weight yarn
- US1 (2.25mm) knitting needles
- 1 pair 2.25 in (6cm) hoop earrings
- (2) french hooks
- Yarn needle
- Scissors
- E6000 glue

shown in:
Be So Fine Yarn; 100% bamboo; 650 yds (594m) per 4oz (113g); color Crushed Berries

Gauge:
24 sts / 24 rows = 4 in (10cm) in garter stitch

Finished Size:
earring is 2.25 in (6 m) diameter when stretched onto hoop earring

Stitch Guide:
See glossary for CO, KCO, knit, kfb and BO.

Instructions:

Earring (make 2):

Row 1: CO 7 sts, kfb in ea st across. -- 14 sts

Row 2: Knit across. -- 14 sts

Row 3: Kfb in ea st across. -- 28 sts

Rows 4 - 6: rep row 2.

BO in picot: *KCO 3 sts, BO 6. Rep from * across, KCO 3 sts, BO all rem sts.

Finishing:
Weave in loose ends. Slide the front (pointy) side of the earring through each of the picots. Evenly slide the picots to cover the entire hoop. Apply a dot of glue to secure each picot to the hoop. Repeat for second earring. Allow to dry completely.

KIMBERLY

Necklace Cowl

This cowl is light and airy but the layers trap warmth nicely. It is a cinch to knit up with icord and pretty little flowers made from a clever combination technique of picots.

What you will need:

- 247 yds (225)m #4 worsted weight yarn
- US8 (5mm) knitting needles, double pointed
- Yarn needle
- Scissors

shown in:
Be So Bold Yarn; 51% organic cotton, 49% bamboo; color Isle D'Amour

Gauge:

12 sts / 16 rows = 4 in (10cm) but gauge is not critical for this project.

Finished Size:

24 in (61cm) circumference

Stitch Guide:
See glossary for CO, KCO, knit, and BO.

Instructions:

CO 2 sts

****Row 1:** slide sts to opposite side of needle, k2.

Rows 2 - 15: rep row 1

*KCO 3 sts, BO 3 sts. Rep from * 3 times, insert needle into horizontal base of each of the 3 picots (4 loops on needle), pass them over the next st on the LH needle.

Rep from ** for desired length. Approx 22 - 24" per loop for necklace. Sample shown is long enough for 13 loops (13x24 = 312 in or 26 feet). Fasten off.

Note: Use a hair clip to manage the length of the icord as you work. It will help to keep everything untangled until you can secure it with the band. Drape necklace around yourself or a dress form until it lays the way you want and secure it.

Band:

Wrap the yarn around all loops together tightly, trying to line up the icord to not have flowers in this section. Either use a crochet hook and single crochet 50 times around all the strands, or just use a tapestry needle and wrap and tie 50 times around all the strands. Either way will work.

Finishing:

Weave in loose ends.

NINA
Shawl

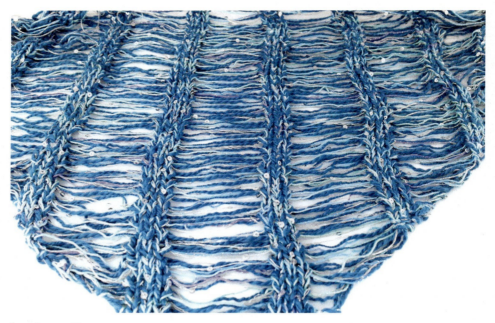

Drop stitches are a fabulous way to show off the texture of beautiful and uniquely constructed yarns. One of the greatest benefits of drop stitches is they grow a fabric exponentially, making this a quick project.

What you will need:

- 140 yds (128m) #6 super bulky yarn, or equivalent with yarns held together
- US8 (5mm) knitting needles
- Yarn needle
- Scissors

Shown in:
Be So Dazzling Yarn; 100% polyester; 100 yds (91m) per 25g spool; color silver

Be So Sporty BLING Yarn; 90% bamboo, 10% silver; 300 yds (274m) per 4oz (113g); color Mermaid 01

Be So Tender Yarn; 100% organic cotton; 140 yds (128m) per 3.5oz (100g); color Lagoon

Gauge:
12 sts / 16 rows = 4 in (10cm) in stockinette stitch

Finished Size:
45 in (114cm) wide x 22 in (56cm) tall

Stitch Guide:
See Glossary for CO, knit, kfb, and BO.

Instructions:

CO 3 sts

Row 1: Kfb, k1, kfb. − 5 sts

Row 2 (and all even numbered rows): K1, purl across to last st: k1.

Row 3: Kfb, k3, kfb. — 7 sts

Row 5: Kfb, k5, kfb. — 9 sts

Row 7 - 65: Kfb, knit across to last st: kfb. — 75 sts

Row 66: BO 3 sts and fasten off. *Drop 3 sts and unravel back to beginning. BO 3 sts, making sure to allow enough yarn to travel the width of the 2 dropped sts, fasten off. Rep from * across.

Finishing:

Weave in loose ends. Hand wash, block to finished measurements and allow to dry.

45 in (114cm)

22 in (56cm)

IRIS

Mobius Cowl

The figure-8 formation of a twisted mobius cowl is simplified with a reversible stitch pattern worked in rows.

What you will need:

- 140 yds (128m) #4 worsted weight yarn
- US6 (4mm) knitting needles
- Yarn needle
- Scissors

Shown in:
Be So Tender Yarn; 100% organic cotton; 140 yds (128m) per 3.5oz (100g); color Fern

Gauge:
16 sts / 20 rows = 4 in (10cm) in pattern

Finished Size:
26 in (66cm) circumference x 8 in (20cm) tall

Stitch Guide:
See Glossary for CO, BO, knit and purl.

Instructions:

CO 33 sts

Row 1: *K3, p3. Rep from * across to last 3 sts: k3. -- 33 sts

Row 2: *P3, k3. Rep from * across to last 3 sts: p3. -- 33 sts

Row 3: Rep row 1. -- 33 sts

Row 4: Rep row 1. -- 33 sts

Row 5: Rep row 2. -- 33 sts

Row 6: Rep row 1. -- 33 sts

Rows 7 - 102: Rep rows 1 - 6 sixteen more times. BO all sts loosely, leaving a long tail. Sew cast on edge to bind off edge, joining corner A to corner D and corner B to corner C per the schematic.

Finishing:

Weave in loose ends. Hand wash, block to finished measurements and allow to dry.

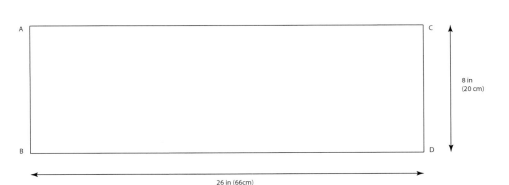

CHELSEA

Washcloth

A reversible combination of stitch patterns adds an interesting geometric design to this washcloth. Make a spa themed gift set with hand knit washcloths, organic bar soaps and some relaxing tea.

What you will need:

- 315 yds (288m) #2 sport weight yarn
- US6 (4mm) knitting needles
- Yarn needle
- Scissors

Shown in:
Be So Bare Yarn; 100% organic cotton; 315 yds (288m) per 4oz (113g); color undyed

Gauge:
16 sts / 28 rows = 4 in (10cm) in pattern

Finished Size:
10 in (25cm) square

Stitch Guide:

See glossary for CO, BO, knit and purl.

Instructions:

CO 40 sts

Note: Slip the first st purlwise at the beginning of each row.

Row 1: K20, (k2, p2)x10. -- 40 sts

Row 2: (K2, p2)x10, p20. -- 40 sts

Row 3: Rep row 1.

Row 4: Rep row 2.

Row 5: Rep row 1.

Row 6: Rep row 1.

Row 7: Rep row 2.

Row 8: Rep row 1.

Row 9: Rep row 2.

Row 10: Rep row 1.

Rows 11 - 35: Rep rows 1 - 10 two more times, then rows 1- 5 once more.

Row 36: (K2, p2)x10, k20. -- 40 sts

Row 37: P20, (k2, p2)x10. -- 40 sts

Row 38: Rep row 36.

Row 39: Rep row 37.

Row 40: Rep row 36.

Row 41: Rep row 36.

Row 42: Rep row 37.

Row 43: Rep row 36.

Row 44: Rep row 37.

Row 45: Rep row 36.

Rows 46 - 70: Rep rows 36 - 45 two more times, then rows 36 - 40 once more. BO all sts loosely.

Finishing:

Weave in loose ends. Hand wash, block to finished measurements and allow to dry.

KHLOE

Small Bowl

If you can make a hat, you can make this visually stunning bowl. A completely hardened, lace knit stitch makes such an interesting home decor accessory. Filling it with contrasting colors really makes the lacework pop. Adding gold leaf to the rim would elevate the elegance or try spray painting the entire bowl with metallic paint.

What you will need:

- 100 yds (91m) #1 fingering weight yarn
- US5 (3.75mm) knitting needles
- Yarn needle
- Scissors
- Smooth-On Smooth-Cast 325 Liquid Plastic
- Latex gloves
- Disposable bowl and stir stick
- Balloon or silicone mold (bowl shaped) with approximately 4 - 5 in (10 - 13cm) circumference

Shown in:
Be So Fine Yarn; 100% bamboo; 650 yds (594m) per 4oz (113g); color Chantilly Lace

Gauge:
16 sts / 16 rows = 4 in (10cm) in pattern

Finished Size:
5.5 in (14cm) diameter x 3 in (7cm) tall

Stitch Guide:
See Glossary for knit, purl, yo, kfb, k2tog, CO & BO.

Instructions:

Set up Row: Make slip knot. Work (k1, p1)x4 into slip knot. -- 8 sts

Row 1 (and all odd numbered rows): knit across.

Row 2: Kfb across. -- 16 sts

Row 4: *K1, yo, k1. Rep from * across. -- 24 sts

Row 6: *K1, yo, k2. Rep from * across. -- 32 sts

Row 8: *K1, yo, k3. -- Rep from * across. -- 40 sts

Row 10: *K1, yo, k4. -- Rep from * across. -- 48 sts

Row 12: *K1, yo, k5. Rep from * across. -- 56 sts

Row 14: *K1, yo, k6. -- Rep from * across. -- 64 sts

Row 16: Knit across.

Row 18: K1, (yo, k2tog)x31, k1. -- 64 sts

Row 20: Knit across

Rows 22 - 40: Rep rows 18 - 20 five more times. -- 64 sts

Rows 41 - 46: Knit across. --64 sts

Finishing:

Cut yarn leaving 18" (45cm) long tail. Thread tail onto yarn needle and sew side edges together. Weave in loose ends.

Saturate in solution per manufacturer's instructions, squeeze out the excess solution, block to bowl shape and allow to dry.

VIVIAN
Small Nesting Basket

This is the smallest of three nesting baskets. The colorful pattern is worked in the round with slip stitch mosaic color technique. Even though the checkered pattern looks complicated, you only use one color of yarn per round!

What you will need:

- 140 yds (128m) #4 worsted weight yarn
- US7 (4.5mm) circular knitting needles, 16 in (40cm)
- Yarn needle
- Scissors
- Stitch marker (optional)
- Crochet Hook (optional)

Shown in:

Be So Tender Yarn; 100% organic cotton; 140 yds (128m) per 3.5oz (100g); color A Cobalt (35 yds/32m), color B Seafoam (35 yds/32m, color C Cloud (35 yds/32m)

Gauge:

20 sts / 24 rows = 4 in (10cm) in slst mosaic colorwork pattern

Finished Size:

4 in (10cm) square base, 4 in (10cm) tall

Stitch Guide

See Glossary for knit, purl, slip stitch, CO and BO.

Instructions:

Base:

With Color B, CO 16 sts

Rows 1 - 32: Knit across. -- 16 sts

Walls:

Round 1: Knit across 16 sts from last row of base, pick up and knit 16 sts along end of rows, pick up and knit 16 sts along cast on edge, pick up and knit 16 sts along other end of rows, join in round. -- 64 sts

Note: If you are new to picking up and knitting, sometimes it is helpful to insert a crochet hook into the specified space, pull up a loop, and transfer it to the knitting needles.

Rounds 2 - 3: With color A, *k2, wyib slip 2 sts. Rep from * around. -- 64 sts

Rounds 4 - 5: With color B, *wyib slip 2 sts, k2. Rep from * around. -- 64 sts

Rounds 6 - 7: With color C, *k2, wyib slip 2 sts. Rep from * around. -- 64 sts

Rounds 8 - 9: With color A, *wyib slip 2 sts, k2. Rep from * around. -- 64 sts

Rounds 10 - 11: With color B, *k2, wyib slip 2 sts. Rep from * around. -- 64 sts

Rounds 12 - 13: With color C, *wyib slip 2 sts, k2. Rep from * around. -- 64 sts

Rounds 14 - 25: Rep rounds 2 - 13 once more. Bind off all sts. Fasten off.

Finishing:

Weave in loose ends. Hand wash, block to finished measurements and allow to dry.

CASSIE

Medium Nesting Basket

This is the middle size of three nesting baskets. The colorful pattern is worked in the round in garter stitch, which is opposite of how you work garter stitch in rows.

What you will need:

- 140 yds (128m) #4 worsted weight yarn
- US7 (4.5mm) circular knitting needles, 16 in (40cm)
- Yarn needle
- Scissors
- Stitch marker (optional)
- Crochet Hook (optional)

Shown in:

Be So Tender Yarn; 100% organic cotton; 140 yds (128m) per 3.5oz (100g); color A Seafoam (70 yds/64m), color B Cobalt (70 yds/64m)

Gauge:

16 sts / 20 rows = 4 in (10cm) in garter stitch

Finished Size:

4.5 in (18cm) square base, 4 in (10cm) tall

Stitch Guide

See glossary for knit, purl, CO and BO.

Instructions:

Base:

With Color A, CO 18 sts

Rows 1 - 36: Knit across. -- 18 sts

Walls:

Round 1: Knit across 18 sts from last row of base, pick up and knit 18 sts along end of rows, pick up and knit 18 sts along cast on edge, pick up and knit 18 sts along other end of rows, place marker, join in round. . -- 72 sts

Note: If you are new to picking up and knitting, sometimes it is helpful to insert a crochet hook into the specified space, pull up a loop, and transfer it to the knitting needles.

Round 2: Purl around. -- 72 sts

Round 3: With color B, knit around. -- 72 sts

Round 4: Purl around. -- 72 sts

Round 5: With color A, knit around. -- 72 sts

Round 6: Purl around. -- 72 sts

Rounds 7 - 34: Rep rounds 3 - 6 seven more times. -- 72 sts

BO all sts. Fasten off.

Finishing:

Weave in loose ends. Hand wash, block to finished measurements and allow to dry.

EVE

Large Nesting Basket

This is the largest of three nesting baskets. They are lovely stand alone gifts or extra special as a trio.

What you will need:

- 140 yds (128m) #4 worsted weight yarn
- US7 (4.5mm) circular knitting needles, 16 in (40cm)
  Yarn needle
- Scissors
- Stitch marker (optional)
- Crochet Hook (optional)

Shown in:
Be So Tender Yarn; 100% organic cotton; 140 yds (128m) per 3.5oz (100g); color Cobalt

Gauge:
16 sts / 20 rows = 4 in (10cm) in garter stitch

Finished Size:
4.5 in (18cm) square base, 5in (13cm) tall

Stitch Guide

See Glossary for knit, purl, CO and BO.

Instructions:

Base:

CO 21 sts

Rows 1 - 36: Knit across. -- 21 sts

Walls:

Round 1: Knit across 21 sts from last row of base, pick up and knit 21 sts along end of rows, pick up and knit 21 sts along cast on edge, pick up and knit 21 sts along other end of rows, place marker, join in round. -- 84 sts

Note: If you are new to picking up and knitting, sometimes it is helpful to insert a crochet hook into the specified space, pull up a loop, and transfer it to the knitting needles.

Round 2: *K1, p1. Rep from * around. -- 84 sts

Round 3: Knit around. -- 84 sts

Rounds 4 - 27: Rep rounds 2 - 3 twelve more times. -- 84 sts

BO all sts. Fasten off.

Finishing:

Weave in loose ends. Hand wash, block to finished measurements and allow to dry.

LANI

Flower Mason Jar Topper

Making decorations for containers filled with gifts is such a lovely sentiment. The 3-dimensional flower is knit flat and sewn to the topper in a spiral.

What you will need:

- 140 yds (128m) #4 worsted weight yarn
- US7 (4.5mm) circular knitting needles 16 in (40cm) length, and double pointed needles
- Yarn needle
- Scissors
- 24 in (61cm) 1/2 in (13cm) wide ribbon

Shown in:
Be So Tender Yarn; 100% organic cotton; 140 yds (128m) per 3.5oz (100g); color Cloud

Gauge:
14 sts = 4 in (10cm)

Finished Size:
Fits a standard Mason jar with 10 in (25cm) circumference

Stitch Guide

See Glossary for CO, BO, knit, k2tog

Instructions:

Flower:

CO 80 sts

Rows 1 - 4: Knit across. -- 80 sts

Row 5: K2tog across. -- 40 sts

Row 6: K2tog across. -- 20 sts

Row 7: Knit across.

BO all sts, leaving long tail for assembly of flower.

Flower assembly:
Wrap strip into a spiral, using photo as your guide for tension of spiral. Using long tail, tack the spiral down on the backside only (where the flower will be a flat surface), allowing for the front to be 3-dimensional.

Topper:

CO 36 sts, join in ring.

Rounds 1 - 2: Knit around.

Round 3: *K2, yo, k2tog. Rep from * around. -- 36 sts

Rounds 4 - 9: Knit around. -- 36 sts

Next Round: K2tog around. -- 18 sts

Next round: K2tog around. -- 9 sts

Pull all sts through tail and cinch. Fasten off.

Finishing:

Sew flower to top center of topper. Weave in loose ends. Weave ribbon through eyelet holes on round 3 of topper.

MIA

Knit Bracelet

The details elevate a simple icord into this stunning bracelet. Loops, knots and a gorgeous Czech glass button bring it all together.

What you will need:

- 100 yds (92m) #2 sport weight yarn
- US6 (4mm) knitting needles (either circulars or double pointed needles)
- Yarn needle
- Scissors
- 35mm Czech Glass Button
- Sewing needle
- Thread

Shown in:
Be So Sporty BLING Yarn; 90% bamboo, 10% silver; 300 yds (274m) per 4oz (113g); color Sunrise 02

Gauge:
16 sts/20 rows = 4 in (10cm)

Finished Size:
7 in (18cm) bracelet

Stitch Guide

See Glossary for knit, kfbf, and k3tog.

Instructions:

CO 1 st

Row 1: Kfbf. -- 3 sts

Row 2: Slide sts to opposite end of knitting needle, k3. -- 3 sts

Rep row 2 until cord is 10 in (25cm) long, k3tog. Fasten off.

Finishing:

With tails, sew ends of icord together to form a loop. Position this seam 1.5 in (3.8cm) from end and join both loops together, to create one long loop and one small loop (see diagram). Sew button to this seam, centered between the two joined cords. Tie a knot in bracelet next to the button, on the longer loop side.

Wrap bracelet around the wrist, insert the longer loop through the smaller loop from the bottom, then up and over the button to secure.

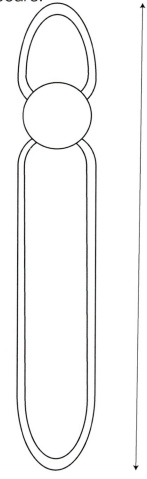

7 in (18cm)

DONNA

Knit Necklace

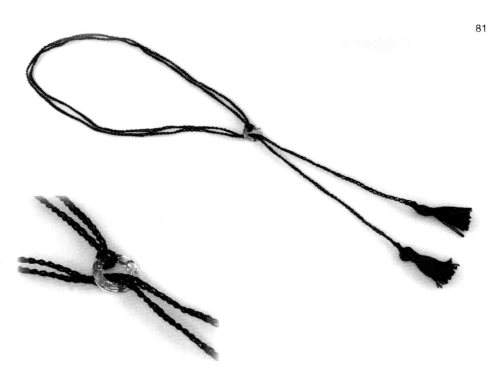

A simple chain is transformed into an elegant lariat necklace with a brilliant Swarovski ring pendant and dainty tassels that give weight and body for a lovely drape.

What you will need:

- 100 yds (94m) #1 fingering weight yarn
- US3 (3.25mm) crochet hook
- Scissors
- Yarn needle
- one 1 in (25cm) Swarovski ring pendant

Shown in:
Be So Fine Yarn; 100% bamboo; 650 yds (594m) per 4oz (113g); color Raven

Gauge:
Gauge is not critical for this project but 32 chs = 4 in (10cm).

Finished Size:
60 in (152cm)

Stitch Guide:
See Glossary for CO and Chain BO.

Instructions:

Chain:
CO 2 sts. Chain BO until chain measures 60 in (152cm). Fasten off.

Tassels (make 2):

Cut 2 pieces of yarn, 12 in (30cm) ea, put aside. Wrap yarn around 3 in (8cm) piece of cardboard 30 times, cut on one side creating 1 bundle of 30 strands. Place bundle evenly between one 12 in (30cm) piece of yarn, tie bundle into place (assuring strands are even). Fold bundle so that strands are even, tie second 12 in (30cm) piece of yarn around bundle, 0.5 in (1.25cm) below knot. Trim bundle ends to make even. Holding two strands of yarn together, secure to end of icord. Weave in ends.

Assembly:
Fold chain in half, and attach to ring with slip knot. Loop tails through ring but do not tighten (this is the loop that will go over the head). Attach the tassels to the ends of each chain with a square knot.

Finishing:
Weave in loose ends.

PAULINA

Knit Cord Necklace

This is a variation of a lariat necklace. It is wrapped twice around the neck for an adjustable choker-style. Knots and beads are added to the ends for texture and drape.

What you will need:

- 150 yds (137m) #2 sport weight yarn
- US6 (4mm) knitting needles, either circular or double pointed needles
- Scissors
- Yarn needle
- (1) 30mm ring pendant
- (4) 8mm x 6mm ornate, large hole spacer charm beads

Shown in:
Be So Sporty BLING Yarn; 90% bamboo, 10% silver; 300 yds (274m) per 4oz (113g); color Sunrise 02

Gauge:
16 sts/20 rows = 4 in (10cm)

Finished Size:
Cord is 60 in (152cm) long

Stitch Guide

See Glossary for CO, knit, kfbf, and k3tog.

Instructions:

CO 1 st

Row 1: Kfbf. -- 3 sts

Row 2: Slide sts to opposite end of knitting needle, k3. -- 3 sts

Rep row 2 until cord is 60 in (152cm) long, k3tog. Fasten off.

Finishing:

Weave in loose ends. Fold cord in half and join to 30mm ring pendant with a slip knot.

Slide 2 beads onto one end of cord. Secure with a knot at tip, slide one bead down to knot, knot again, slide second bead down to knot, knot again. You should have 3 knots separated by 2 beads at end of cord. Repeat for other end of cord.

BRIDGET

Knit Wire Bracelet

Knitting with wire makes sophisticated jewelry. The drawplate is the secret to getting even and professional stitches. Use caution when choosing knitting needles for this project because wire can scratch softer finishes like wood and bamboo. I suggest using metal knitting needles.

What you will need:

- 100 yds (91m) 28 gauge wire
- US2 (2.25mm) metal double pointed needles, set of 5
- Yarn needle
- Scissors
- (1) draw plate
- Sewing needle
- Waxed beading thread
- (1) 1 in (25cm) magnetic closure with 3 holes

Shown in:

28 gauge wire; 109 yds (99m) per spool, color silver.

Gauge:

32 sts/32 rows = 4 in (10cm) after running through drawplate

Finished Size:

7.5 in (19cm) long x 1.5 in (4cm) wide

Stitch Guide

See Glossary for CO, BO, and knit.

Instructions:

CO 24 sts, divide evenly over 4 needles (8 sts each), join in round, leaving long tail.

Round 1: Knit around. - 24 sts

Rounds 2 - 78: Repeat round 1. Fasten off, leaving long tail.

Finishing:

With tails, cinch cast on edge and bind off edge to narrow the ends of the tube.

Pull tube through drawplate, starting with the largest hole and gradually sliding through the smaller holes until you get a smooth, uniform finish to your stitches.

Flatten the tube into a 2-sided piece 7.5 in (19cm) long x 1.5 in (4cm) wide.

Note: If you don't have a drawplate, smooth the stitches with a rubber mallet and your fingers as you flatten the tube for a similar effect.

Weave in wire tails. Using sewing needle and thread, sew each end of wire cuff to the two pieces of the bracelet closure, making sure to line up the closures correctly. When lying flat, one side will face up and the other will face down.

EDEN
Punch Cards

Not only are handmade cards a treat to receive, but a set of handmade cards also makes a lovely gift. Make them in assorted colors and tie together with a bow.

What you will need:

- Stationery, 4 in (10cm) x 6 in (15cm), folded
- Paper punch 'lace edge' 4 in (10cm)
- Paper punch 'flower' 1/2 in (13cm)
- Paper punch 'love' 3 in (7cm)
- Contrast cardstock 65lb
- Glue stick
- Scissors
- Bone folder for crisp, sharp edges if making your own cards

Finished size:
4 in (10cm) x 6 in (15cm), folded

Note: Any size card or stationery can be used for this project.

Instructions:

1. Using lace edge paper punch, cut out lower edge of front of card. When card is wider than punch, carefully line up punch overlapping first punch when punching out again.

2. Cut a piece of cardstock 1 in (25cm) taller than the punch out, and cut to the exact width of the card.

3. Punch 'love' out of cardstock.

4. Punch flowers out of cardstock.

5. Glue 'love' to center front of card. Glue flowers to each side of 'love'. Glue cardstock lining to back of front of card, underneath the lace cut out.

Make these in assorted colors for a set of 6 or 12.

JULIA
Knit Embellished Card

A simple knit flower adds another dimension to a handmade card. Make a set of these for the knitter you love.

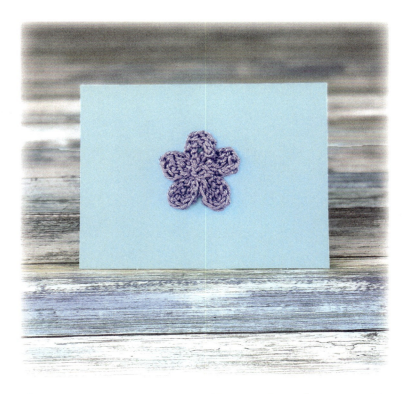

What you will need:

- 50 yds (45m) #2 sport weight yarn
- US3 (3.25mm) knitting needles
- Yarn needle
- Scissors
- Stationery, 4 in (10cm) x 6 in (15cm), folded
- Glue stick
- Bone folder for crisp, sharp edges if making your own cards

Shown in:
Be So Sporty Yarn; 100% bamboo; 325 yds (297m) per 4oz (113g); color Lilac Memories

Finished size:
4 in (10cm) x 6 in (15cm), folded

Note: Any size card or stationery can be used for this project.

Instructions:

CO 45 sts

Row 1: *K1, BO 8. Rep from * across. -- until 5 sts remain

Cut yarn, leaving long tail. With yarn needle, weave through remaining 5 sts and remove from knitting needle. Cinch tightly and secure. *Working between petals, wrap yarn around flower and back up through center. Rep from * for all petals. Weave in loose ends.

Glue flower to center front of card.

LENORA
Crochet Card

A simple crochet flower adds another dimension to a handmade card. Make a set of these for the crocheter you love.

What you will need:

- 50 yds (45m) #1 fingering weight yarn
- D/3 (3.25mm) crochet hook
- Yarn needle
- Scissors
- Stationery, 4 in (10cm) x 6 in (15cm), folded
- Glue stick
- Bone folder for crisp, sharp edges if making your own cards

Shown in:
Be So Fine Yarn; 100% bamboo; 650 yds (594m) per 4oz (113g); color Chantilly Lace

Finished size:
4 in (10cm) x 6 in (15cm), folded

Note: Any size card or stationery can be used for this project.

Instructions:

Ch5, slst to 5th ch from hook to form ring.

Round 1: ch6 (counts as dc, ch3), (dc, ch3)x5 in ring, slst to 3rd ch at beg of round to join.

Round 2: (sc, 3dc, sc) in ea ch3 sp around, slst to first st at beg of round to join. Fasten off. Weave in loose ends.

Glue flower to center front of card.

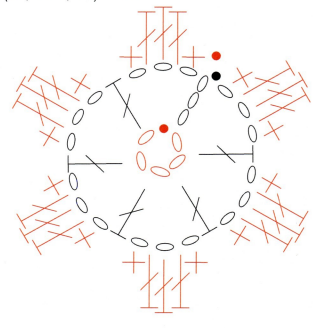

GINA
Heat Embossed Cards

Heat stamp embossing is a really elegant and deceptively simple technique for creating sophisticated stationery gifts.

What you will need:

- Stationery, 4 in (10cm) x 6 in (15cm), folded
- Stamps
- Versamark stamp pad
- Embossing powder, gold
- Multi-purpose embosser heat tool
- Bone folder for crisp, sharp folds if making your own cards

Finished size:
4 in (10cm) x 6 in (15cm), folded

Note: Any size card or stationery can be used for this project.

Instructions:

1. Choose a clean, dry stamp to begin.

2. Press stamp into Versamark ink pad.

3. Press stamp onto card in desired space.

4. Sprinkle embossing powder over mark left by stamp. Make sure you cover it completely.

5. Let the excess powder slide off of card onto a separate sheet of paper. Flick card with fingers to clean as much of the excess powder from card as possible. A cotton swab or paintbrush is helpful, too. The excess powder can now be returned to the container for future use.

6. Hold the embossing tool about 6 in (15cm) away from the image. Sweep over image, taking care to not stay in one spot too long. As the embossing powder melts, it will become smooth, shiny and dimensional.

Note: It is important not to use the embossing tool near any loose powder: the embosser will blow the powder around and make a mess.

SOPHIA
Heart Box

These adorable little boxes could be filled with anything from a sentimental note to jewelry. Or fill a box with a handmade truffle.

What you will need:

- 1 sheet 110lb cardstock
- X-Acto knife
- Bone folder for crisp folds
- Pen
- Glue

Finished size:
2.5 in (6cm) wide x 2.5 in deep (6cm) x 3 in (7cm) tall

Instructions:

1. Trace template.

2. Cut cardstock along solid lines on template with X-Acto knife.

3. Gently fold along each dotted line.

5. Gently slide slot over two longer sides. Then repeat with second slot.

6. Curl each of the two exposed tabs above the slots, rolling around a pen to face the curled edges inward.

7. With a dot of glue, join the two curved edges of the tabs to form a little heart.

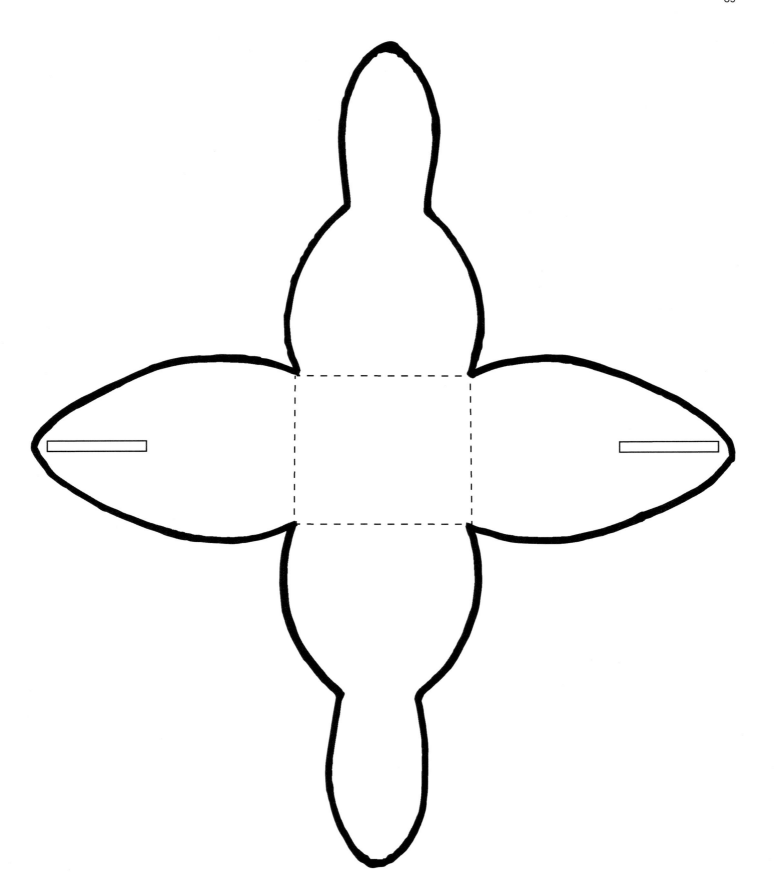

AUGUSTA
Woven Baskets

Woven baskets can be a gift on their own, but they also make a fantastic container for other gifts, too! Fill a woven basket with stationery, yarn, wash cloths, or anything you desire.

What you will need:

- Yard stick
- Roll of kraft paper, 24 in (61cm) wide
- Scissors
- Glue stick

Finished size:

small: 2 in (5cm) wide, x 2 in (5cm) deep x 4 in (10cm) tall
large: 3 in (7cm) wide, x 3 in (7cm) deep x 3 in (7cm) tall

Note: Any size basket can be made as long as you use the same number of strips vertically as you use horizontally when making the base.
Each round of strips to create the walls will be the circumference of the base plus 1 in (2.5cm) for seam.

Instructions:

1. Take roll of kraft paper, and wrap tightly around yard stick seven times. Cut.

2. Repeat step 1 to create as many base strips as you require. The small basket will use 4 base strips and the large basket will use 6 base strips.

3. Weave the base of the basket. Lay out 2 (3) strips vertically. Add a strip horizontally alternating it over and under the vertical strips. Add a second (and third) horizontal strip, working it over and under the vertical strips opposite the previous strip. Slide the woven part to the very center so all four sides of strips are equal in length.

4. Fold and crease each side across the base to make a bend in the strips.

5. Cut out as many strips as you want height for your basket. The small basket uses four strips 9 in (23cm) long and the large basket uses three strips 13 in (33cm) long. Repeat step 1 for these strips.

6. Fold the wall strips in four positions: every two (three) inches from edge. There should be one inch left over. Glue the one inch overlap to the beginning of the strip. Repeat for all wall strips. You should now have four (three) wall rings.

7. Fold up every other base strip vertically and slide the wall ring over and down to the base. *Fold those strips back down and fold up the opposite strips. Slide the next wall ring over and down to the last wall ring. Repeat from * until your walls are complete.

8. Fold the remaining vertical strips over the wall rings, and glue to secure. Every other one can be secured to the interior of the basket or the space between the two layers of the walls.

HENRIETTA
Origami Box

This box is simple to fold and magically transforms into a gorgeous box. Decorate with ribbons or yarn for closure and use stickers or shapes punched out of contrasting paper for added variety. The schematic notes the direction and position for adding decorations.

What you will need:

- 12 in (30cm) square 78lb cardstock
- Bone folder for scoring crisp folds in paper
- Paper hole punch, 1/4 in (6mm)
- Paper punch, 1/2 in (13cm)
- 18 in (47cm) 1/2 in (13cm) ribbon or
- Crochet chain with fringe
- Shown in **Be So Tender Yarn** color Lagoon wtih 3 in (7cm) fringe with H/8 (5mm) crochet hook
- Contrasting color cardstock

Finished size:
4 in (10cm) square base, 3 in (7cm) tall

Instructions:

1. Fold diagonally from corner to corner, open and then repeat for opposite corners (yellow lines on chart).

2. Fold horizontal center line, and fold from edge to center line in each direction. Turn paper and repeat. (red lines on chart)

3. Fold from corner to opposite red intersecting lines. Repeat for all four sides (purple lines on chart).

4. Fold each corner to adjacent red intersecting lines (green lines on chart).

5. Using paper punch, make holes in paper along purple lines 1/2 in (13cm) from edge (make 8 holes).

6. Fold yellow/green corner inward, and fold purple/purple lines together inward, press and release. Thread ribbon or chain through holes and slowly cinch as you re-fold. As box is slowly cinched, the folds will take hold.

7. Punch out decorative flowers and stars with contrasting cardstock.

8. Add the decorations to the boxes with a drop of glue.

Note: The schematic shows the eight exposed sides of the box labeled as A through H, with arrows pointing up in case you need to position your decorations with direction.

Optional Crochet Chain and Fringe:

Make a crochet chain 30 in (76cm) long. Fasten off.

Cut 8 pieces of yarn 4 in (10cm) long. Take 4 strands and fold in half. Insert crochet hook into last chain at end of crochet chain and pull the strands partially through. Make a slip knot. Repeat for fringe on second end.

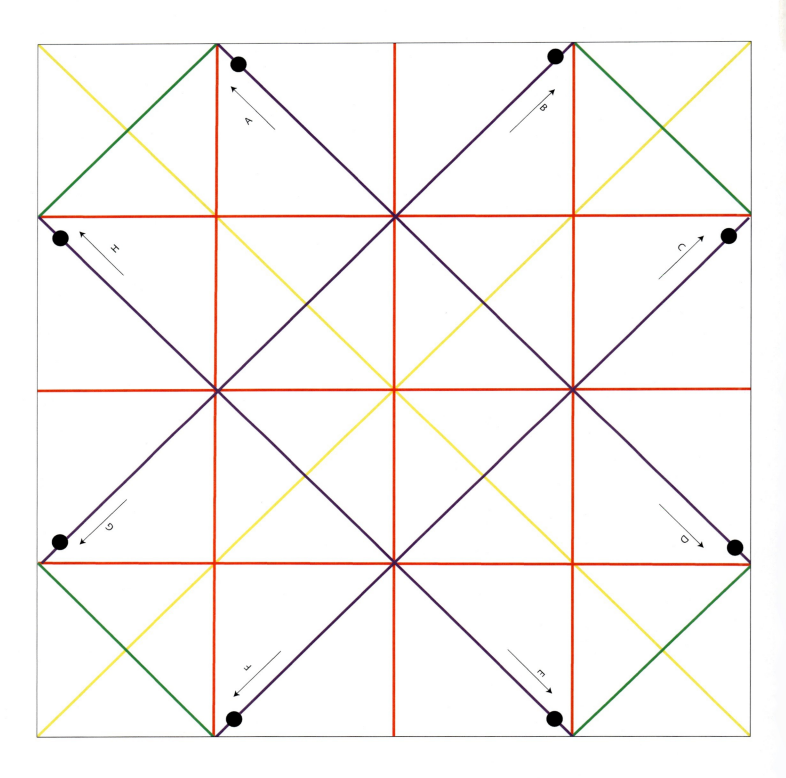

VICTORIA
Pillow Box

A pillow box is a simple way to add a personal touch to anything from a gift card to jewelry. Add stickers, stamps, punched out shapes, a calligraphy message or drawing to make it even more special.

What you will need:

- 1 sheet 110lb cardstock
- X-Acto knife
- Bone folder for scoring paper
- Scissors
- Glue

Optional:
- Paper punches, shown in 1 in (25cm) and 1/2 in (13cm) sizes
- Contrasting color cardstock

Finished size:
6 in (15cm) long x 3 (7cm) in wide

Instructions:

1. Trace template.

2. Cut cardstock along solid lines on template.

3. Score along dotted lines on template.

4. Gently fold along each dotted line.

5. Glue flap along long side of box and allow to dry.

6. Put slight pressure on the folded lines along the long sides of the box to pop out the sides (to create the pillow shape).

7. One at a time, fold the curved edges inward. If necessary, glue or tape to secure.

8. Decorate the boxes with stickers, stamps, punched out shapes or any other kind of decoration. You can also secure with a ribbon and tie a bow.

Note: Use holiday cards or birthday cards you've received to make these. They would be pre-decorated and just as easy to make.

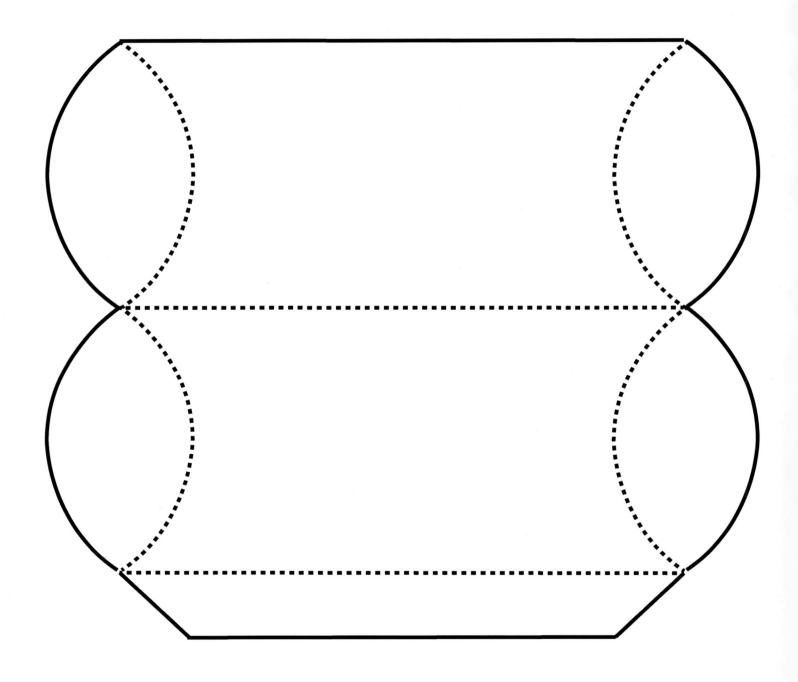

CASSANDRA

Fabric Box

This pretty box makes a great gift presentation when filled with goodies. Can you imagine using a selection of these for organization in your craft room, office, or linen closet? So pretty!

What you will need:

- (4) 22 in (56cm) square cotton bandanas, 2 each in 2 different colors
- or (4) 22 in (56cm) squares of cotton fabric
- 2 yds (1.8m) medium weight fusible interfacing
- Steam iron
- Sewing machine
- Pins
- Fabric shears

Finished size:

6 in (15cm) x 12 in (30cm) base, 6 in (15cm) tall

Instructions:

1. Iron interfacing to one side of each square of fabric following manufacturer's instructions.

2. With right sides together in same color fabric, sew 1/2 in (13cm) seam around perimeter, leaving 4 in (10cm) unsewn.

3. Trim corners being careful not to cut through seams. Turn right side out. Sew the 4 in (10cm) space closed by hand or with sewing machine. Press with iron.

4. To create boxed corners, fold each corner with seam down the center. Mark 3 in (7cm) perpendicular from point; sew. Cut excess fabric to 1 in (2.5cm) from new seam. Repeat for second corner.

5. Repeat steps 2 - 4 for second color fabric.

6. With outer fabric wrong side facing out, and inner fabric sitting inside outer fabric, right sides facing, pin upper hem together. Sew around perimeter, leaving 4 in (10cm) unsewn.

7. Turn right sides out. Sew the 4 in (10cm) space closed by hand or by machine. Press with iron.

Note: A shoe box fits into the base and can help in shaping for ironing.

PEARL

Pinafore Apron

Pinafore aprons are useful for all types of crafters. Make one for the gardener, baker, chef, artist or woodworker in your life.

What you will need:

- Two pieces of fabric cut 24in x 48in (body) or 60cm x 121cm
- Two pieces of fabric cut 24 in x 5 in (straps) or 60cm x 12cm
- Eight pieces of fabric cut 8 in (20cm) x 12 in (30cm) for pockets
- Fabric shears
- General sewing machine supplies

Note: These specifications of fabrics will create a reversible apron; pockets on the two sides can be added to match or contrast. Choose your prints accordingly.

Instructions:

1. Cut all fabrics to size.

2. Iron all fabrics.

3. Pin 2 pocket pieces of fabric together, right sides facing. Sew 1/2 in (1.3cm) seam allowance around entire perimeter, leaving 5 in (13cm) opening for turning right side out. Repeat for second pocket (2 pockets on front). Repeat for 3rd and 4th pockets if you are putting pockets on the reversible side of the apron.

4. Cut excess fabric in corners to help make the corners crisp, being careful not to cut into or through the seams. Turn right sides out. Use a chopstick or other bluntly pointed object for popping the corners. Press with iron. Sew up the 5 in (13cm) opening.

5. With right sides facing, pin pockets symmetrically to fronts of both body pieces, per diagram.

Note: Decide whether you are using contrasting or matching pockets for each side of the body. Top stitch around the sides and bottom of each pocket, attaching to the body piece, with a 1/4 in (6mm) seam allowance.

Note: Make sure you don't sew across the tops!

6. Sew each strap piece lengthwise with a 1/2 in (1.3cm) seam allowance. Turn right side out and press seams open with iron so the seam is lined up in the

center (back side) of each strap. Repeat for second strap. Fold raw edges of narrow ends inward and press with a 1/2 in (1.3cm) seam allowance.

7. Pin the two body pieces of fabric together, right sides facing. Sew 1/2 in (1.3cm) seam allowance around entire perimeter, leaving 5 in (13cm) open for turning right side out.

Note: Leave the opening on the lower edge.

8. Cut excess fabric in corners to help make the corners crisp. Turn right sides out. Use a chopstick or other bluntly pointed object for popping the corners. Press with iron.

9. Top stitch 1/4 in (6mm) seam allowance around perimeter of body pieces, turning and pressing a 1/2 in (1.3cm) seam allowance inward at the 5" opening edges before sewing.

10. Sew straps to apron with a fortified square and x detail for security and durability. Line up first strap centered over pocket, and the second end of same strap over opposite side's corner. Repeat for second strap. (See diagram for placement).

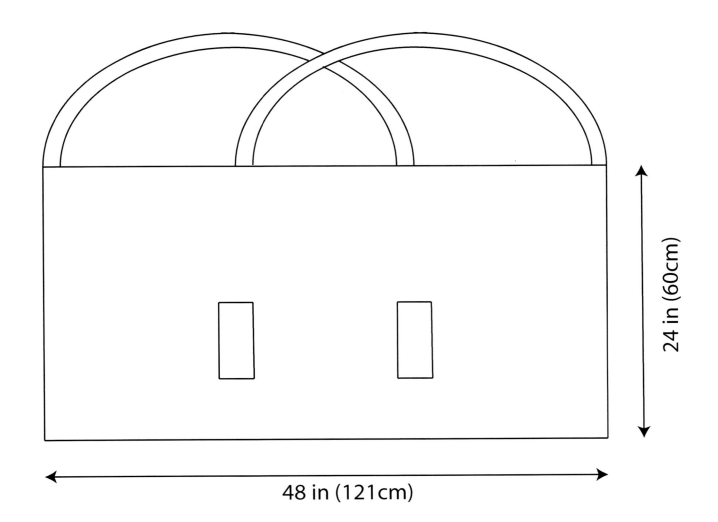

HEATHER
Jelly Roll

This makes a quick and fabulous gift! Use this for crochet hooks, double pointed knitting needles, coloring pencils, markers or makeup brushes.

What you will need:
- Three pieces of cotton fabric, 16 in (40cm) x 10 in (25cm)
- One piece of medium weight fusible interfacing 15 in (38cm) x 9 in (23cm), optional
- 36 in (91cm) of 1/2 in (13cm) grosgrain ribbon
- or
- 36 in (91cm) crochet chain and fringe
- Pins
- Sewing machine

Finished size:
15 in (38cm) x 9 in (23cm)

Note: Crochet chain and fringe are shown in **Be So Sporty Yarn** in color Passionate Plum

Note: This is easily customized to any size. Simply cut your fabrics to the desired size, and your interfacing 1 inch (2.5cm) smaller on each side.

Instructions:

1. Cut fabrics to size. Press them smooth. Line the outer fabric with interfacing, if you choose. The roll-up cases are equally as nice with or without the interfacing.

2. Fold one piece of fabric in half lengthwise (this is the pocket). Press it smooth.

3. Pin the pocket piece to the fabric you chose for the inside of the roll (right sides facing).

4. Pin the ribbon tie (at the halfway point) to the outer edge of the inside fabric (just above the join of the pocket to the inside fabric).
 Note: Make sure the ribbon is facing inward on the right side of the fabric.

5. Lay the fabric you chose for the outside of the roll on top of the previously assembled pieces, making sure the right sides are facing.
Note: You should now see the wrong side of this fabric facing up.

6. Pin all fabrics together at corners.

7. Sew the perimeter of the fabrics together, keeping 3 - 4 in (7 - 10cm) unsewn at the top of the roll (the opposite of the pocket.

8. Trim the corners of the fabrics (make sure you don't cut your seams). This will allow for the corners to be more crisp when you turn the fabrics right side facing out.

9. Turn the roll to right sides facing out. Press them smoothly. Fold the hem of the opening to the inside to match the rest of the seams.

10: Carefully sew a top stitch 1/4 in (6mm) around perimeter of roll (making sure you catch the pressed seam of the opening as you go. Go slowly at the corners for a smooth finish.

11. Mark the fabric at 1 in (2.5cm) intervals (or whatever intervals you prefer for your pockets). 1in (2.5cm) is great for crochet hooks and coloring pencils. 1.5 in (3.5cm) might be better for markers or make up brushes.

12. Sew vertical lines along the entire roll, starting at pocket and working toward top. Backstitch at beginning and end of each line of stitches.

REESE

Drawstring Bag

Lining a bag is a big step toward a professional-looking finished project. A flat bottom allows the bag to sit up on its own, which is great for a knitting or crochet project bag. The exterior drawstring casing adds an additional pop of color.

What you will need:

- Two pieces of cotton fabric 12 in (30cm) x 30 in (76cm), one print for bag and one for lining
- Two pieces of fabric cut 9.5 in (24cm) x 3 in (7cm) (preferably the lining fabric print or a third print)
- Fabric marker
- Pins
- Sewing machine
- Iron
- Fabric shears
- Thread
- Safety pin
- Two pieces of 1/2 in (1.3cm) grosgrain ribbon cut 30 in long

Finished size:
5 in (12cm) square base x 12 in (30cm) tall

Instructions:

1. Cut fabrics to dimensions and press with iron.

2. Fold the two smaller pieces of fabric in half lengthwise and press. Open up, then fold each edge toward the center crease and press again. The width should be 1.5 in (3.5cm) now.

3. Fold the side edges 1/2 in (1.3cm) and press. Sew this edge to secure.

4. Pin the drawstring casings to the exterior bag fabric, 3 in (7cm) down from the edge. Working parallel to the short sides of the fabric. Sew along both long lengths of the drawstring casing, 1/4 in (6mm) from edge.

Note: Do not sew over the short edges of the casing again. These must remain open for the drawstring.

5. Fold both of the large pieces of fabric in half widthwise. Pin sides and sew 1/2 in (1.3cm) seam allowance from fold to edge.

6. Press the side seams open so they come to a point and the seam runs down the center of the point.

7. With a fabric marker, mark a line perpendicular to the seam 2.5 in (6cm) from point. This will be the gusset that makes the bottom of the bag flat.

8. Sew along line. Make sure to back stitch at beginning and end.

Note: Make sure the gussets are pressed and sewn identically otherwise your bag may not sit perfectly flat.

9. Cut points off, leaving 1/2 in (1.3cm) of fabric before seam. Do not cut seam!

10. Turn exterior bag right

side facing out. Insert it into the lining bag (with right side facing in). The right sides of the fabric should be facing in and touching. And the wrong sides of the fabric should be facing out. Pin together, making sure to line up the seams.

11. Sew 1/2 in (1.3cm) seam allowance around, leaving 4 in (10cm) unsewn.

12. Pull the bags through the hole, right sides facing out.

13. Insert the lining bag into the exterior bag. Press seams. Press the opening hem to match the rest of the sewn hem.

14. Sew 1/4 in (6mm) seam allowance around the top of the bag, making sure to catch the unsewn opening.

15. Thread the ribbons through the drawstring casing as follows: Attach a safety pin to one end of one ribbon. Thread it through the drawstring casing on one side of the bag and then through the other side of the bag's casing. Both ends of the ribbon will be on the same side. Remove the safety pin and tie these ends in a knot. Attach a safety pin to one end of the second piece of ribbon. Thread it through the drawstring casings same as the first ribbon EXCEPT begin and end on the opposite side of the bag. Tie these ends into a knot.

16. Trim any excess ribbon ends.

The bag will cinch tightly when you pull on the knots on both sides of the bag at the same time. And it will stand up!

SASHA

Stitch Markers

Stitch markers make a wonderful gift for both knitters and crocheters. This particular style is well suited for both kinds of crafters because they can be opened and closed. Presenting the gift on a bangle bracelet not only looks cute but is also great for storage.

What you will need:

- Assorted charms
- 6mm jump rings
- (2) pair chain nose pliers
- 27mm x 14mm lobster clasps
- One 2.4 in (6cm) Expandable Blank Bangles Bracelet

Finished size:
Varies, depending on size of charm.

Instructions:

1. Firmly hold the jump ring with pliers on either side of the seam (seam at top). Twist the wire front to back until the required opening is achieved.

2. Holding ring with one set of pliers, insert charm and lobster clasp onto opened ring at the same time.

3. Hold ring with two sets of pliers same way as for opening, and gently twist the ring back into place. Because the wire is springy, you may need to "rock" the pliers back and forth past the seam until the ring remains closed. You should be able to achieve a very flush close.

4. Using lobster claw, open and attach to expandable blank bangle bracelet.

EMILY

Eye Pillow

I first saw an eye pillow many years ago while working in a luxurious spa. It wasn't long before I began making my own and giving them to my friends and family. I still love to give them to friends when they need a little pick-me-up.

What you will need:

- One piece of fabric cut 12 in (30cm) x 10.5 in (26cm)
- Sewing machine
- Thread
- Fabric shears
- 2 cups (300g) dry rice, flaxseeds, or corn
- 1 TBSP (15ml) dried lavender buds
- Funnel or rolled up sheet of paper

Instructions:

1. Cut fabric to size.

2. Press smoothly.

3. Fold in half lengthwise with right sides together. Pin perimeter.

4. Sew along three sides: one short side, turn and sew along long side, turn, and sew along short side. Leave 3 in (7cm) open for adding the rice and lavender. Backstitch at the beginning and end.

5. Cut the corners, but do not cut into the seams!

6. Turn the bag right side out. Using a chopstick or knitting needle really helps to make the corners crisp!

7. Press smoothly. Turn the hem of the opening to match the rest of the seams.

8. Mix the rice and lavender together.

9. Fill the bag no more than halfway with the rice mixture.

Note: A funnel or rolled up sheet of paper can be helpful here.

10. Sew a 1/4 in (6mm) top stitched seam along both of the short sides of the bag.

ALICE

Reversible Tote Bag

This FABULOUS bag is easy to make. Use it for a knitting or crochet project bag, taking to the market, on a picnic, travel, or even use it as your purse! Makes a wonderful gift for a baby shower, bridal shower, or birthday filled with all kinds of goodies.

What you will need:
- 1/2 yard (.45m) cotton fabric (outer bag)
- 1/2 yard (.45m) complementary cotton fabric (lining)
- 1/2 yard (.45m) fusible interfacing (medium weight)
- 44 in (112cm) canvas strap webbing, cut into two 22 in (56cm) pieces
- Pins
- Steam iron
- Sewing machine
- Fabric Shears
- Thread

Finished size:
12 in (30cm) tall x 19 in (48cm) wide at top, base is 12 (30cm) wide x 6 (15cm) deep

Instructions:

1. Cut Fabrics
Cut two 20" x 15" rectangles of outer fabric, inner fabric and interfacing. Cut webbing into two 22" pieces.

2. Snip corners. On the long side of all 6 rectangles (2 outer fabric, 2 lining fabric and 2 interfacing), cut a 3 x 3 in (7 x 7 cm) corner from only the bottom corners.

3. Press interfacing to wrong side of outer fabric rectangles, following manufacturer's instructions.

4. With right sides together, sew the sides and bottom together of outer fabric. Leave the top and two snipped corners unsewn. Repeat for lining fabric pieces. Press seams open.

5. Sew corners. Pinch together the gaps in the snipped corners, lining up the side and bottom seams in the center. Sew 1/2 in (1.3cm) seam. This step creates a flat bottom. Repeat for lining fabrics.

6. Flip liner right-side out and place inside outer fabric so that right sides are facing each other. Tuck the straps between the inner and outer fabrics. You want two edges of one strap facing the front and two edges of the other strap facing the back of the bag. You also want them centered and mirroring each other. Begin each strap approx. 4 in (10cm) from side seam. Pin all pieces together, and make sure you line up the side seams as well.

7. Beginning at a side seam, sew 1/2 in (1.3cm) seam around perimeter of bag, leaving a 4 in (10cm) opening from the starting point. Make sure you catch all 4 straps, while leaving enough room to turn the entire bag out through the opening.

8. Pull both fabrics and both straps through the opening. Turn the bag right-side out and tuck the lining into the bag. Press top seam with iron, and turn the opening's hem inward to match the rest of the seam.

9. Top stitch around the entire bag's opening to finish the edge, making sure to close the opening. This also reinforces the canvas straps.

ANNIE

Velcro Pouch

A little velcro pouch has so many possibilities. Add it to a project bag, fill it with notions, or use it in a thousand other ways. I have shown it filled with a hank of yarn.

What you will need:

- (2) pieces 16 in (40cm) x 8 in (20cm) cotton fabric (preferably one each in two different prints
- (2) pieces 16 in (40cm) x 8 in (20cm) medium weight fusible interfacing
- Sewing machine
- Fabric marker
- Dinner plate
- Fabric shears
- Pins
- Iron
- 1 in (2.5cm) fusible Velcro

Finished size:

7 in (18cm) wide x 6 in (15cm) tall

Instructions:

1. Iron interfacing to wrong side of all fabrics, following manufacturer's instructions.

2. Draw curved line along one short edge of all fabrics using a dinner plate as guide. Cut along line.

3. With right sides facing, pin both fabrics together. Sew around perimeter, leaving 4 in (10cm) opening.

4. Turn right side out, pushing corners with chopstick or other blunt object to make crisp corners. Press with iron.

5. Sew 1/4 in top stitch along short flat edge.

6. With right side facing out, fold flat edge over until 3.5 in (9cm) from curved edge.

6. Pin. Starting from one folded corner, sew a 1/4 in top stitch along doubled edge, around curve, and back down over doubled edge to other folded corner.

7. Using fabric marker as guide, match up spots on front of pouch and underside of curved flap for Velcro.

8. Cut 1 in of Velcro. Remove lining from adhesive side and affix Velcro pieces to marked positions on pouch and flap.

9. Heat with iron according to package directions. Allow to cool completely.

ADA
Cord Keeper Roll

This is a fantastic gift for the travellers in your life. Whether a daily commuter, college student or international globe-trotter, a pretty and soft roll for organizing electronics and cords is a thoughtful and functional gift.

What you will need:

- Two pieces of cotton fabric 12 in (30cm) x 24 in (60cm)
- Two pieces of medium weight fusible interfacing 12 in (30cm) x 24 in (60cm)
- 4 in (10cm) fusible Velcro
- 36 in (91cm) crochet chain plus 3 in (7cm) fringe, shown in **Be So Tender Yarn**; #4 worsted weight organic cotton yarn; color Seafoam
- H/8 (5mm) crochet hook
- B/1 (2.25mm) crochet hook
- (3) pieces of 1/2 in (13mm) elastic, 10 in (25cm) long

Finished size:
16 in (40cm) long x 11 (28cm) in wide, flat

Instructions:

1. Iron fusible interfacing to wrong side of both fabrics, following manufacturer's instructions.

2. Pin elastic lengthwise along center of lining fabric, 1 in (2.5cm) from top edge. Pin second and third elastics parallel with 3 in (7cm) spacing on either side of center elastic.

3. Sew across elastic at both edges and in 3 in (7cm) increments. In the top segment of the 3 in (7cm) sections, add seams at 1 in (2.5cm) increments.

4. Pin right sides of fabric together. Sew 1/2 in (13cm) seam around perimeter, leaving 4 in (10cm) opening.

5. Turn right side out. Press with iron. Sew up the 4 in (10cm) opening.

6. Fold one short side up 6 in (15cm) from edge. Pin. **Note:** Not the side with the elastic sewn onto it.

7. Starting at one folded corner, sew 1/4 in (6mm) top stitch down along long side, across bottom, and up the second long side, ending at second folded corner. Backstitch at the beginning and end.

8. With H/8 (5mm) crochet hook and yarn, chain 80. With smaller crochet hook B/1 (2.25mm), push through fabric at center of top narrow side of roll. Hook last loop worked and pull through. Put loop back on larger crochet hook and chain 80. Fasten off.

9. Cut four 6 in (15cm) pieces of yarn for fringe. Add to one end of chain. Repeat for second end of chain.

10. Remove adhesive lining on both sides of Velcro and affix to the interior of pocket, centered 1/2 in (13) from edge of pocket.

11. Heat with iron according to package directions. Allow to cool completely.

MARGOT

Zipper Pouch

Zipper pouches are easy and quick to make. They can be used for anything from storing notions to jewelry. They can be used as a gift bag or given as a gift themselves in a set of coordinating prints. Alternate your lining and exterior prints for a set. The possibilities are endless.

What you will need:

- Four pieces of 7 in (18cm) x 7 in (18cm) cotton fabric, two each in different prints for exterior and lining fabrics
- One 7 in (18cm) zipper
- Pins
- Sewing machine and zipper foot

Finished size:
6 in (15cm) square

Note: This pouch can be modified to make any size. Just make sure your zipper is as long as the width of your fabric.

Instructions:

1. Make sure you use the zipper foot on your sewing machine.

2. Place the zipper right sides facing with outer fabric and pin. Sew the zipper to the fabric.

3. Repeat step two for other side of zipper and other piece of outer fabric.

4. Sandwich one long edge of the zipper between a piece of lining and the outer fabric already sewn to it. Stitch again, along the same stitched line of the outer fabric with the right sides together and zipper sandwiched between them.

5. Repeat step four for other side of zipper and other piece of lining fabric.

6. Unzip the zipper most of the way. Fold the pouch so that the outer fabrics are right sides together and the lining fabrics are right sides together.

7. Pin fabrics making sure to match the outer fabrics at the zipper and fold the zipper teeth toward the lining.

8. Sew around the perimeter leaving 4 in (10cm) unsewn at the bottom of the lining.

9. Cut across the corners, but be careful not to cut the stitching.

10. Turn right side out. Use a blunt object, like a chopstick, to turn the corners crisply.

11. Top stitch along the hole left in the bottom of the lining.

12. Turn the lining inside the pouch. Press with iron.

GRETA

Bath Bombs

This is a simple recipe for making bath bombs: they are chock full of amazing ingredients to relax your muscles and elevate your bathtub to a luxurious spa treatment. When you perfect popping the bath bombs out of the molds, you will have gorgeous, handmade gifts to give anyone! I have yet to meet a person - man or woman - who doesn't love my bath bombs.

What you will need:

- 1 cup (299g) baking soda
- 1/2 cup (100g) cornstarch
- 1/2 cup (100g) citric acid
- 1/4 cup (50g) Dead Sea salts
- 1/4 cup (50g) Epsom salts
- 2.5 TBSP (40ml) Avocado oil
- 1 TBSP (15ml) water
- several drops fragrance oil or essential oil
- Several drops food coloring (optional)
- Silicone molds, shown in 3 in (7cm) x 1 in (2.5cm) discs

Finished size:
3 in (7cm) x 1 in (2.5cm) discs

Yield: 6 discs per batch. With smaller molds, you can get more units per batch.

Instructions:

1. Combine and mix all dry ingredients in a large bowl.

2. In a separate bowl, mix together all the wet ingredients before adding to dry ingredients.

3. Combine the dry and wet ingredients together and mix thoroughly. The consistency should be like moist sand.

4. Pack densely into molds.

5. Leave to dry at least 24 hours, and up to 72 hours depending on your humidity, before popping out of molds.

Note: If you attempt to pop them out too soon, they will crumble. Even though crumbled bath bombs are not pretty for gifts, be sure to collect all of this as it is still perfectly wonderful for your own baths!

Symbol Library

- • slip stitch (slst)
- o chain (ch)
- ⊗ ch3 picot
- + single crochet (sc)
- T half double crochet (hdc)
- ⊥ half double crochet (through back loop only)
- 4 double crochet cluster (4dc-cl)

- ∤ double crochet (dc)
- foundation oval
- 2 double crochet cluster (2dc-cl)
- 3 double crochet cluster (3dc-cl)
- 3 double crochet together (dc3tog)

- 2 treble crochet cluster (2tr-cl)
- 3 treble crochet cluster (3tr-cl)
- 4 double crochet cluster (4dc-cl)
- ∤ treble crochet (tr)

Crochet Glossary

2-tr cluster (2tr-cl): Yarn over twice, insert hook in next specified stitch, yarn over, pull up a loop, (yarn over, pull through 2 loops on hook)x2. *Yarn over twice, insert hook in same stitch and pull up a loop, (yarn over, pull through 2 loops on hook)x2, (3 loops on hook). Yarn over, pull through all 3 loops on hook.

3-tr cluster (3tr-cl): Yarn over twice, insert hook in next specified stitch, yarn over, pull up a loop, (yarn over, pull through 2 loops on hook)x2. *Yarn over twice, insert hook in same stitch and pull up a loop, (yarn over, pull through 2 loops on hook)x2. Rep from * once more (4 loops on hook). Yarn over, pull through all 4 loops on hook.

4-dc cluster (4tr-cl): Yarn over, insert hook in next specified stitch, yarn over and pull up a loop. Yarn over, pull through 2 loops on hook. *Yarn over, insert hook in same stitch, yarn over and pull up a loop. Yarn over and pull through 2 loops on hook. Rep from * two more times (5 loops on hook). Yarn over, pull through all 5 loops on hook.

Adjacent (adj): Next to or adjoining something else.

Bead Chain: Slide strung bead snug up to work, chain 1.

Beg 3tr-cluster: Ch4, *yox2, insert hook in next specified stitch, yo, pull up a loop, (yo, pull through 2 loops on hook)x2. Yarn over twice, insert hook in same stitch and pull up a loop, (yo, pull through 2 loops on hook)x2. (3 loops on hook). Yo, pull through all 3 loops on hook.

Chain (ch): Wrap the yarn over the hook in a clockwise direction. Draw the yarn through to form a new loop without tightening the previous one.

Ch3 picot (ch3 picot): Ch3, slst to 3rd ch from hook.

Ch5 Join: Ch2, slst to ch5 sp on adjacent motif, ch2.

Ch7 Join: Ch3, slst to ch7 sp on adjacent motif, ch3.

Double Crochet 3 Together (dc3tog): [Yo, pull up a loop in indicated st or sp, yo and draw through 2 loops] 3 times, yo and draw through all 4 loops on hook.

Double Crochet (dc): Wrap the yarn over the hook and insert the hook into the work (or specified chain from hook), wrap the yarn over the hook, draw through the work only and wrap the yarn again. Draw through the first two loops only and wrap the yarn around the hook again. Draw through the last two loops on the hook.

Double Treble Crochet (dtr): Wrap the yarn over the hook three times and insert the hook into the work (or specified chain from hook). Wrap the yarn over the hook, draw through the work and wrap around the hook again. Draw through the first 2 loops only and wrap the yarn around the hook again. (Draw through the next two loops only and wrap the yarn around the hook again) x2. Draw through the last two loops.

Foundation Oval (ch4, dc): *Ch4, dc in fourth ch from hook. Rep from * for desired length.

Half Double Crochet (hdc): Wrap the yarn over the hook and insert the hook into the work (or specified chain from hook), wrap the yarn over the hook, draw through the work only and wrap the yarn again. Draw through all three loops on hook.

Picot Join: Ch 1, slst to adjoining motif's picot, ch 1, slst to specified stitch.

Single Crochet (sc): Insert the hook into the work (or specified chain from hook), wrap the yarn over the hook and draw the yarn through the work only. Wrap the yarn around the hook again and draw it through both loops.

Slip Stitch (slst): Insert hook into specified stitch. Wrap the yarn over the hook. Draw the yarn through the stitch and through the loop on the hook.

Treble Crochet (tr): Wrap the yarn over the hook twice and insert the hook into the work (or specified chain from hook). Wrap the yarn over the hook, draw through the work and wrap around the hook again. Draw through the first 2 loops only and wrap the yarn around the hook again. Draw through the next two loops only and wrap the yarn around the hook again. Draw through the last two loops.

Through back loop (tbl): Work the specified stitch(es) through the back loop only.

Tunisian double crochet:
Row 1: Chain to desired length, *yo, insert hook in 3rd ch from hook, yo, pull up a loop, yo, pull through 2 loops on hook. Rep from * in ea ch across. Return: yo, pull through 1 loop on hook. *Yo, pull through 2 loops on hook. Rep from * across.
Row 2: Ch2, skip first elongated stitch, *yo, insert hook in next elongated stitch, yo, pull up a loop, yo, pull through 2 loops on hook. Rep from * across. Return: yo, pull through 1 loop on hook. *Yo, pull through 2 loops on hook. Rep from * across.

Knitting Glossary

3 Needle Bind Off: Place the stitches to be joined onto two separate needles and hold the needles parallel so that the right sides of the knitting face together. Insert a third needle into the first stitch on each of two needles and knit them together as one stitch. *Knit the next st on each needle the same way, then use the left needle tip to lift the first stitch over the second stitch and off the needle. Repeat from * until no stitches remain on first two needles. Fasten off and pull tail through last loop to secure.

Bind Off: Knit 2 stitches, then lift the first stitch over the second stitch and off the needle. *Knit 1, then lift the first stitch over the second stitch and off the needle. Repeat from * for desired number of stitches.

Cast On: Place thumb and index finger on your left hand between the yarn ends so that working yarn is around your index finger and tail end is around your thumb and secure the yarn ends with your other fingers. Hold your palm upward, making a V of yarn. *Bring needle up through loop on thumb, catch first strand around index finger, and go back down through loop on thumb. Drop loop off thumb and placing thumb back in v-configuration, tighten resulting stitch on needle. Rep from * for desired number of stitches.
Note: Unless otherwise specified, this is the bind off technique used throughout this book.

Chain BO: *Bind off one stitch, yarn over, pull the first stitch over the yarn over as if to bind off. Repeat from * for desired lenth of chain.

Knit (k): Insert needle from front to back into next stitch on left needle. Wrap yarn and draw through to complete stitch and slip the new stitch to the right needle.

Knit 2 Together (k2tog): Insert needle into next 2 stitches at the same time and knit, (1 decrease).

Knit 3 Together (k3tog): Knit 3 stitches together, (2 decreases).

Kfb: Knit into the front and back of the stitch, (1 increase).

Kfbf: Knit into the front, back and front of same stitch, (2 increases).

Knit Cast On (KCO): Insert the right needle into the stitch and work a knit stitch, but do NOT slip it off of the left needle. Tilt the right needle to the right and insert the left needle into the loop you've pulled up. Repeat for desired number.

Pick up and knit: *With right side facing and working from right to left, insert the tip of the needle into the center of the stitch below the bind off or cast on edge, wrap yarn around needle, and pull through a loop. Repeat for desired number of stitches.

Purl (p): Insert needle from back to front into next stitch on left needle. Wrap yarn and draw through to complete stitch and slip the new stitch to the right needle.

Yarn Over (yo): Yarn over needle.

Kristin Omdahl is committed to helping survivors of domestic violence and shedding light on this frightening and often hidden crime in our society. In an attempt to achieve these goals and help eradicate domestic violence, Kristin will donate a portion of the proceeds from this book and all Kristin Omdahl products to the fund she established: Project Kristin Cares. All funds collected by Project Kristin Cares will be donated to help survivors of domestic violence.

Resources

DxO One
dxo.com
DxO One Camera

Eucalan, Inc.
eucalan.com
Wrapture all natural, no-rinse delicate wash

Kristin Omdahl Fabrics
spoonflower.com/profiles/kkomdahl
Day of the Dragonfly Collection

Kristin Omdahl Yarns
kristinomdahl.com
Be So Bare, Be So Bold, Be So Brave, Be So Dazzling, Be So Fine, Be So Fresh, Be So Serene, Be So Tender, Be So Sporty, and Be So Sporty BLING Yarns

Findings, tools & machines:
amazon.com/shop/kristinomdahl

Full detailed list of all resources:
www.KristinOmdahl.com/80Handmade Gifts

Please visit **KristinOmdahl.com** for a massive library of video tutorials for every technique used in this collection, plus more!

Right hand, left hand and slow motion visual instructions are available with closed captioning subtitles.

Index

2-tr cluster 24
3-tr cluster 24, 41, 43, 45
3 needle BO 65
4-dc cluster 29
Abigail Bag 29
Acknowledgements 3
Ada Roll 105
Amanda Necklace 57
Alice Bag 103
Asian Pickled Green Beans 14
Annie Pouch 104
Arianna Earrings 70
Augusta Basket 90
Baklava Balls 7
baking powder 12
banana 9
bead chain 36
beans, green 14
Belle Napkin 33
bind off (BO) 63, 66, 68, 69, 70, 71, 72, 73, 74, 75, 76, 77, 78, 79, 83
blueberries 9, 12, 22
Bridget Bracelet 83
butter, salted 8, 18
Caliope Bag 65
Cami Scarf 34
caramel candies 21
cardamom 5, 12, 22, 23
Carly Napkin 68
Caroline Candle Holder 51
Carrie Bag 66
carrots 14
Cashew Cream Cheese 20
Cassandra Box 95
Cassie Medium Basket 77
cast on (CO) 63, 65, 66, 68. 69, 70, 71, 72, 73, 74, 75, 76, 77, 78, 79, 81, 82, 83
Celeste Earrings 35
ch5 join 31
ch7 join 24
Chai Spice 5
chain (ch) 24, 27, 29, 31, 33, 35, 36, 39, 41, 43, 45, 47, 49, 51, 53, 56, 57, 58, 59, 60, 62
Chain CO 81
cheese, cheddar 17, 18
Cheese Crackers 18
cheese, cream 17
Cheese Log 17
Chelsea Washcloth 74
chili powder 6
chili flakes, red 10
chives 17
chocolate, melting 16
chocolate chips, semi-sweet 8, 16, 21
Ciara Scarf 69
cilantro 14
cinnamon 5, 6, 7, 21, 22
cloves 5, 6, 22

Cocoa Mixes 21
cocoa powder 21
coconut 4, 7
coffee, instant 21
Courtney Bowl 67
cranberries 4
cream, heavy 16
cucumbers 14
cumin 6, 14
Dana Earrings 62
dates 7
dc3tog 47, 53
double crochet (dc) 24, 27, 29, 31, 33, 36, 39, 41, 43, 45, 47, 51, 53, 59, 60, 62
Dedication 3
Donna Necklace 81
double treble crochet (dtr) 62
Eden Card 84
eggs 12
Emily Eye Pillow 102
Eve Large Basket 78
Felicia Mobius Cowl 38
Flavored Sugars 22
flour 18
food coloring 9
foundation oval 24, 27
Gabi Candle Holder 53
garlic, fresh 10, 11, 14
Garlic Oil 10
garlic, powder 14
Gina Card 87
ginger 4, 6, 14, 22, 23
glossary 108, 109
Grace Bracelet 55
Granola, Chai Spiced 4
Greta Bath Bombs 107
half double crochet (hdc) 27, 38, 47, 51, 53
Heather Roll 98
Henrietta Box 91
horseradish 14
Hope Case 27
Introduction 3
Iris Mobius Cowl 73
Jennifer Bowl 31
Julia Card 85
k2tog 63, 65, 66, 67, 68, 75, 79
k3tog 63, 67, 80, 82
Kate Trivet 41
knit cast on (KCO) 70, 71
Kelly Earrings 59
kfb 63, 70, 72, 75
kfbf 63, 80, 82
Khloe Bowl 75
Kimberly Necklace Cowl 71
knit (k) 63, 65, 66, 67, 68, 69, 70, 71, 72, 73, 74 75. 76, 77, 78, 79, 80, 82, 83
Lani Jar Topper 79
lavender buds, dried 9, 22
Lemon Blueberry Mini Loaf

Cakes 12
lemons 9, 11, 12, 17, 22
Lenora Card 86
Lexi Washcloth 39
Line Raspberry Loaf Cake 12
limes 12, 22, 23
Liz Necklace 58
Maggie Bag 63
Margot Pouch 106
Marlene bag 24
marshmallows 21
Melanie Candle Holder 49
Mia Bracelet 80
milk, non-fat dry 21
Mimi Candle Holder 47
Moroccan Pickled Carrots 14
mustard seeds 14
Nicole Washcloth 45
Nina Shawl 72
nuts, almonds 4, 6
nuts, cashews 6, 20
nuts, mixed 8
nuts, macadamia 6
nuts, pecans 4, 8
nuts, walnuts 7
oats 4
oil, olive 10
oil, sesame 14
Oil, vegetable 12
Olivia Shawl 36
onion powder 14
onion, red 23
Orange Cardamom Mini Muffins 12
oranges 9, 11, 12, 22
oregano 10
parsley 17
Paulina Necklace 82
paprika, smoked 6, 18, 19
peaches 11, 23
Peach Chutney 23
Pearl Apron 96
pepper, black ground 5, 17, 19
pepper, cayenne 6, 17, 21, 23
pepper, jalapeno 14
peppers, red bell 14
peppermint candies 21
pick up and knit 66
picot join 31
pineapple 4, 22
pistachios 6, 17
Project Kristin Cares 110
purl (p) 63, 65, 66, 67, 68, 73, 74, 75, 76, 77, 78
quinoa 19
Quinoa Crackers 19
Rachel Necklace 56
raspberries 11, 12, 22
Raspberry Vinegar 11
Reese Bag 99
Resources 110
rose petals 9, 22

rose water 7
rosemary 10
salt, Himalayan pink 6, 12, 14, 19, 20 21, 23
Sami Trivet 43
Sasha Stitch Markers 101
seeds, chia 19
seeds, hemp 19
seeds, sesame 19
single crochet (sc) 24, 27, 29, 31, 33, 35, 39, 41, 43, 45, 47, 49, 51, 53, 58, 59, 60, 62
Simple Syrups 9
slip stitch (slst) 24, 29, 31, 33, 39, 43, 45, 47, 49, 51, 53, 55, 56, 59, 60, 62, 76
Sophie Box 88
Spiced Nuts 6
star anise 5, 22
strawberries 11, 22
sugar, light brown 4, 6, 23
sugar, confectioners 12
sugar, white 8, 9, 12, 14, 21, 22
Sweet Pickled Relish 14
Symbol Library 108
Tanya Jar Topper 60
thyme 10, 11
treble crochet (tr) 24, 60, 62
Truffles 16
through back loop (tbl) 38, 55, 56
Toffee 8
Tunisian dc 34
vanilla extract 12, 16
Victoria Box 93
vinegar, apple cider 14, 23
vinegar, rice wine
vinegar, white wine 11
Vivian Small Basket 76
yarn over 65, 69, 75
yeast, nutritional 19
yogurt, non-dairy 20
yogurt, plain dairy 12

Longing for more inspiration from Kristin?

Look no further.

KristinOmdahl.com

@KristinOmdahl

Other titles by Kristin Omdahl:

80 Handmade Gifts, 2018
Create Share Inspire, Volume I, Issues 1 - 5, 2018
Crea Comparte Inspira, Volumen I, Periódicas 1 - 5, 2018
Layers, Volume 1, 2018
Motif Magic, Volume 1, 2018
Continuous Crochet, 2016
Crochet So Lovely, 2015
Zen Art: A Coloring Book, 2015

I Taught Myself to Knit 18" Doll Clothes, 2015
I Taught Myself to Crochet 18" Doll Clothes, 2015
Beginners Guide to Knitting in the Round, 2014
Knitting Outside the Swatch, 2013
The Finer Edge, 2013
Complements Collection, 2012
A Knitting Wrapsody, 2011
Seamless Crochet, 2011
Crochet So Fine, 2010
Wrapped In Crochet, 2008

Made in the USA
Columbia, SC
02 November 2018